LATE CUTS

VIC MARKS
LATE CUTS
Musings on Cricket

ALLEN&UNWIN

First published in Great Britain in 2021 by Allen & Unwin

This paperback edition first published in Great Britain in 2022
by Allen & Unwin

Allen & Unwin
c/o Atlantic Books
Ormond House
26–27 Boswell Street
London WC1N 3JZ

Phone: 020 7269 1610
Fax: 020 7430 0916
Email: UK@allenandunwin.com
Web: www.allenandunwin.com/uk

A CIP catalogue record for this book is available from the British Library.

Paperback ISBN 978 1 83895 306 5
E-Book ISBN 978 1 83895 305 8

Printed and bound in Great Britain by Clays Ltd, Elcograf S.p.A.

10 9 8 7 6 5 4 3 2 1

Contents

Preface

WELCOME TO A work in progress. It's time to find a title. That can't be too difficult, can it?

Just as they say never judge a cricketer by watching him in the nets, so we should never judge a book by its cover. But suddenly I'm not so sure about that. When Javed Miandad was watching the teenage Wasim Akram in the nets in 1984 or Misbah ul-Haq was casting an eye over an even younger Naseem Shah in 2019, they both decided straightaway that they wanted to catapult these young fast bowlers into the national team. And clearly they were right to trust their gut instincts. It only took them a glance to reach their conclusions.

So perhaps the title – and the cover – matter after all, which sends the mind into a giddy top spin that prevents any coherent thought – or the discovery of a decent title. Ah... Top Spin? How about that? A sort of sequel to *Original Spin*, which I hope you enjoyed. I know there is a slippery slope out there populated by tired cricket book titles and I have started sliding down it. I am staring at some of them. For wicket-keepers The Gloves Are (always) Off; for former captains there are Final Declarations; those retiring gracefully sign off with Over and Out. Someone is always Following On. This is going to be trickier than I thought. The Americans seem to do this so much better: *To Kill a Mockingbird, Catcher in the Rye, One Flew Over the Cuckoo's Nest*. Now these are proper titles and extraordinary books. Which came first, I wonder?

For the very first time I'm experiencing some sympathy with the architects of The Hundred, who decided they had to come up with exciting titles for the eight squads they created in their brainstorming session in some darkened room at the offices of the England and Wales Cricket Board. Now I can just about see how, in desperation, they got to 'Welsh Fire' for a squad that was supposed to embrace the counties of Gloucestershire and Somerset as well as Glamorgan and which, after the first draft of players had been completed in 2019, contained no Welshmen at all. 'Trent Rockets' still sounds like a perma-tanned, soft-porn actor of the 1960s. As for the other names of the teams in the competition, I'm afraid I can't remember them despite a barrage of publicity from the ECB.

The Hundred has not yet captured my imagination. It is a competition that has become increasingly derided – and increasingly superfluous – except for those employed at considerable expense to play, coach, broadcast and administer it, all of whom think it is a jolly good idea (and here are my bank details). Moreover, it is sponsored by a company that produces junk food in abundance at a time when obesity is an ever more dangerous and prevalent problem. As cricket seeks to restore its roots after the Covid-induced devastation of 2020, this is what I'm supposed to be excited about.

What follows here was triggered by Covid-19. Don't worry,

it does not dwell long on the pandemic – or The Hundred, for that matter. The lockdown that began in March 2020 eventually drove me to the laptop and I had ample time to return there at the end of the year during the third lockdown. There was nowhere to go and not much to do. Soon after the start of the first lockdown I was asked to keep a very brief fortnightly diary. On 3 April I noted, 'The novelty [of the lockdown] soon wore off, as did the determination to read Shakespeare, Dickens and Joyce. Within a week all the fine ideas of self-improvement slithered away as a new routine evolved. Initially I became a news junkie, soaking up every detail; for a few days those 5 p.m. press conferences from Downing Street became compulsory viewing. But enthusiasm for that did not last long either... as the passing on of vital guidance and information was increasingly replaced by barely concealed attempts to justify the handling of the problem.'

I added that 'the 2020 edition of *Wisden*, published later this week, will not mention the disease because it erupted too late to be included. The glorious cricketing summer of 2019 is therefore unsullied.' I decided that I would be better off turning my mind to something I knew about in an attempt to escape the deepening gloom that was evident from an entry of 2 May: 'What is clear – and this may be a surprise to some of the arch-Brexiteers – is that we are no better, and arguably worse, at dealing with this pandemic than our European neighbours despite the wisdom of Chris Whitty, the one I instinctively trust whenever I watch those afternoon press conferences.'

So during that lockdown I started writing about cricket

and not Covid (though I was briefly taken by the title Covid's Metamorphoses). After six decades consumed by the game, this was my specialist subject. Whether what follows turns out to be therapy for me or entertainment for you remains to be seen. To achieve both outcomes would be a bonus.

Initially it looked as if there would be no cricket at all in the summer of 2020 so there would be plenty of time to contemplate various aspects of the game and to write about them. But then the ECB, despite its self-destructive obsession with The Hundred, reacted with a rare mix of flexibility and creativity that was in stark contrast to their attempts to woo women and children to their wondrous new competition. They undertook to deliver international cricket behind closed doors with Steve Elworthy, who had overseen what now seemed like the straightforward task of organizing a 50-over World Cup in 2019, to the fore. First and foremost the ECB needed the money from their lucrative TV deal to diminish the size of the losses caused by the pandemic, but there was also the nobler urgency to keep the game alive. And they did it.

They had to overcome a range of unprecedented obstacles, which began with persuading the government and the touring teams that cricket was safe and feasible behind closed doors. There was no cricket anywhere in the country until the second week of July, which left us correspondents endlessly debating whether it would ever happen and whether it would be worthwhile if it did. We rarely bothered to consider what might constitute England's best bowling attack or who should open the batting, since such topics seemed of secondary importance and maybe there was no point in giving any attention to such minutiae anyway. There might be too many hurdles to over-come for any cricket to take place.

Suddenly being a cricket correspondent had become a solitary profession. There were no press boxes to inhabit, no gossip, no random cricket chat. In fact, in the summer of 2020 I did not see any of my writing colleagues until 8 September at the first T20 fixture against Australia in Southampton. When attending Test matches or ODIs before then, I was in a different bubble – the broadcasters' inner bubble rather than the outer one occupied by the writers – and under no circum-stances were we allowed to mingle. However, when the Test series against the West Indies began on 8 July 2020, I was on my sofa. The cricket was on the television and this was the only way to watch it except for a hundred or so workers at the Ageas Bowl, the out-of-town home of Hampshire CCC. I settled down with a coffee and a mixture of anticipation and trepidation. I was hungry for some cricket to report – after all, this was how I was supposed to earn a living – but I was fearful the game would not work in a deserted, sterile stadium. And then it rained and this was magical.

The Test match was taking place in the wake of the death of George Floyd in Minneapolis, which had prompted protests all around the globe from Black Lives Matter. Sky TV caught the mood brilliantly. Their audience tuned in eagerly for the novelty of some live sport but, after all the intricate prepara-tions, rain was going to delay the start. So Sky played a superb, pre-recorded fifteen-minute piece featuring Michael Holding and Ebony Rainford-Brent. The film began with a quote from James Baldwin: 'Not everything that is faced can be changed, but nothing can be changed until it is faced,' and from this point onwards we were transfixed.

Both Michael and Ebony spoke candidly of their early experiences in the game and the prejudice, at times unwitting, that they had endured along the way. It was impossible to desert the screen. This was potent stuff way beyond the scope of any normal sports broadcast. Michael was Michael: eloquent, heartfelt but also open to an extent that even surprised some members of his own family. And we saw a different Ebony. Her default position in all the time she has decorated radio and TV commentary boxes has seen her with a constant, beaming smile, twinkling eyes and a light-hearted, optimistic view of the world. But here the eyes were moist and the smile was gone as she recounted the ingrained prejudice she had come across in her years as a young cricketer.

My coffee went cold and the rain continued to fall at Southampton. So Sky's presenter, Ian Ward, followed on by hosting a live conversation on a balcony at the Ageas Bowl. By now Michael was off his long run – and, as we all know, he had the most graceful of long runs the game has ever seen. He delivered a memorable monologue that ranged from Judas Iscariot to the inventor Lewis Howard Latimer. Nasser Hussain was alongside him and spoke for many of us: 'People will be tuning in and saying: "Not this again." All I'll say to those people who say "not again" is that a few weeks ago I watched a black man being killed in front of my eyes on *Channel 4 News* and my natural reaction was to look away. Next time that footage came on, I forced myself to watch because I felt something inside of myself say: "You've been looking away too long."' Hussain is a private man but his barriers had been blown away. He did not even pretend he had been watching the horrors in Minneapolis on Sky News rather than Channel 4.

Well, this was so much more mesmerizing than watching Dom Sibley bat. But for the rain, I might have missed half an hour of the most riveting television imaginable. The players of both sides took the knee before the start. On that first day only 17.4 overs were bowled; England were 35-1 at the close but the series and a bizarre summer of international cricket had been well and truly launched. And everyone was talking about it – or at least they were talking about the candid recollections of Michael and Ebony.

The rain did not go away for long in the late summer of 2020, but when it relented we were treated to some surprisingly compelling cricket. I watched the first two Tests from the sofa before entering the inner bubble at Old Trafford for the third match against the West Indies. By now I had an ECB passport hidden away somewhere on my phone, upon which I had to log the absence of any coughs and sneezes during the previous twenty-four hours and without which it was impossible to gain entry to the ground. Already I had been tested at the ECB's considerable expense. My tester drove from Cardiff to Exeter, a journey of about two and a quarter hours. He put a swab in my throat and up my nose, which took about thirty seconds, whereupon he turned around and went back to Wales.

Upon arrival at Old Trafford it took a while to get to the hotel that overlooks the ground, which was where the players and the broadcasters were staying. Naturally, locating and operating the Covid passport on my phone was the first obstacle and it required expert assistance from a medic, who fortunately possessed sufficient IT skills. Then I was given my 'inner bubble' accreditation, plus a tag that would monitor my every movement while on the site, and there were strict instructions that both the accreditation and the tag should be worn constantly. In stark contrast to the rest of the country, a 'world-class' track-and-trace operation was already up and running within the confines of the Old Trafford bubble.

In the car park a chicane had been constructed that led to the first thermal tent. I got out of the car, flashed my new accreditation and then was finally able to drive around to the hotel. Before entering, there was another temperature tent to go through, then another check of my accreditation. Finally I was inside and my heart was sinking. At reception and in the nearby dining area there were masks, pale-blue rubber gloves and Perspex screens everywhere. From behind one of those a friendly receptionist signed me in, disinfected my little suitcase and eventually handed over a key before I headed off to my room/cell. By now I was pining for my own sofa.

In fact the room was one of the better ones (I think it had been occupied by a knight of the realm, Sir Alastair Cook, during the previous Test) since it faced the ground rather than the car park. I was informed that, on health and safety grounds, it would not be serviced during my stay. How could such a venerable broadcaster possibly survive in such squalor? Soon I was briefed by a BBC assistant producer about the rules relating to masks, social distancing and dining procedures before she warned 'and, whatever happens, keep away from the turquoise arrows. They are for the players only.' All around the Old Trafford complex there were arrows of different colours on the tarmac, which indicated where everyone was allowed to walk. Apparently I was only permitted on the yellow ones. To step on the turquoise ones might mean exile.

Just after my arrival at the hotel I saw a couple of players in a corridor near my room; I could briefly greet Jack Leach. But this was obviously an aberration; it should not have happened. Indeed it did not happen again. The broadcasters and the players were completely separated even though we were staying in the same hotel. Then I went to the media centre on the other side of the ground, where the broadcasters – but not the writers, who were situated on the top tier of the pavilion throughout the game – were stationed, in order to find the *Test Match Special* commentary box, where I had been asked to contribute to a preview of the match.

The sign outside the box declared 'Maximum of Five People Permitted'. The producer, Adam Mountford, had his workplace at the back of the box, a chair and a table bearing vital bits of machinery all surrounded by Perspex. On the other side of the room this was mirrored by the berth of Andy Zaltzman, the scorer/statistician and the one genuine comedian in the team. The commentary positions at the front of the box were socially distanced; we all had our own set of microphones and we could use no others. Only I could touch my microphone, which may explain some of the unusually long delays in commentary when I was handing over to the next summarizer. It took a while to master plugging myself in and out.

Initially this was all very depressing. I had descended into some dystopian world in order to watch a dozen white-clad figures running around an empty stadium and going through some arcane and incomprehensible (to the majority of the world's population) ritual out on the grass during the breaks in the rain. Back at the hotel it was time for dinner and at last a little light was shed. I was surprisingly pleased to see my broadcasting colleagues. I had been in lockdown for almost four months and here was a gathering of familiar, mostly smiling faces who did not seem at all bothered by the bizarre restrictions that had been imposed upon them. Having already broadcast two Test matches, this was all routine to them; they had evolved a matter-of-fact acceptance that this was the way it was. We sat at our individual, socially distanced tables and ate and chatted more loudly than normal. Within a couple of hours I was also managing to adjust to this strange new normal amid the odd realization that I had communicated with far more people on that first evening at Old Trafford than had been the case throughout the previous four months in Devon.

Somehow the cricket worked behind closed doors. And it worked especially well during the Test matches. The games kept coming and it was as if they were replacing the television soap operas that had run out of episodes due to the lockdown. Characters emerged from the cameras, some of whom were not household names: on the West Indies side was Jason Holder, an impeccable leader, forever vibrant and smiling; there was Jermaine Blackwood, impishly attempting lofted drives that were not supposed to happen in Test cricket; there was also Shannon Gabriel, bustling up to the crease and bowling fast before retreating to mid-on, where he seemed barely capable of moving at all in between his overs. For England there was Sibley, with a batting style that even Heath Robinson would have rejected as being too quirky, and he was becoming something of a folk hero. Ben Stokes, now a Test captain, had already achieved this status, while Stuart Broad's renaissance was becoming a source of wonder. To the little seam of viewers on Sky television and many more watching the BBC highlights, they all became familiar characters. On the radio the commentary may have provided some compensation for the absence of *The Archers*, who all seemed to be on furlough.

The cricket took over to the extent that we started to fret about England's top three again rather than whether the series would be completed. After the West Indies' first Test victory at the Ageas Bowl the outcome was always in the balance. A month later the first Test against Pakistan delivered the most compelling cricket of the summer at Old Trafford in a game that England were losing until the final afternoon when Jos Buttler and Chris Woakes joined forces in spectacular style.

So it became apparent that Covid-19 had produced a little silver lining. All the restrictions had seemed certain to diminish any sporting contests to the point that they may as well be written off as a waste of time and energy. Yet, despite all the obvious limitations, Test match cricket was offering up an engrossing product and a rather better one than most other sports could deliver. Covid was doing the game a favour. And so were the players of all the international sides who were prepared to come to England in 2020. As the cameras zoomed in, it was obvious that they all cared hugely about the outcome of the matches, that they respected the game and their opponents, and with barely an aberration they also respected the confines of their bubbles, which proved to be beyond some of the big names in other sports.

The white-ball games followed suit. Ireland, after two desultory defeats to England at the Ageas Bowl, emulated their famous Bangalore victory of 2012, though they did it rather more quietly this time. Then the advent of Australia for six white-ball matches in September delivered what suddenly seemed to be a sequence of unmissable clashes. It helped that an engaging England side demonstrated a melodramatic never-say-die attitude. They had come back from probable defeat against Pakistan in the first Test, and they did the same in two games against Australia, which cheered just about everyone up. On both occasions the cameras latched on to a grim-faced Justin Langer, Australia's head coach. He cared all right. No surprise there, but so did everyone else as the glum faces of the Australians and the beaming smiles of the England players, who had just picked their pockets, confirmed.

All this served as a reminder that somehow the game still mattered. Test cricket was perhaps the greatest beneficiary. Those matches in July and August provided a surprisingly gripping escape from the pandemic while the white-ball formats also offered a welcome end-of-season diversion before the football saturation took over.

There would soon be spectacular confirmation of the magic of Test cricket, when India toured Australia in December and January. In the first Test at Adelaide, India were bowled out for 36 and lost by eight wickets. Their captain, Virat

Kohli, as planned, then left the tour to become a father. The pundits, all the usual suspects in the Australian commentary boxes, and the odd Englishman (who does not like to be outdone) predicted a clean sweep for the Aussies. Ajinkya Rahane took over the captaincy from Kohli rather brilliantly and, despite a catalogue of injuries to senior members of his bowling attack, India contrived to win, 2-1, late in the final session of the final day at the Gabba where Australia had not lost for thirty-two years.

The series had provided breathtaking drama to lift the spirits. 'Thanks, India. Thanks a lot. What else can you say? Thanks for one of the classic series. Thank you for one of the more extraordinary days. When Washington Sundar, a 21-year-old stripling on Test debut, hooks the best Australian fast bowler of his generation for six to give this match and series its final wrench, what other can you say?' wrote Greg Baum, who always seems to catch the mood, in *The Age*. Then England's victory over India in Chennai in the first Test startled an unusually large television audience back at home after Channel 4 had won the rights – three days before the series began. The millions who rely only on free-to-air television for their sport could see for themselves why Joe Root was being hailed as a minor genius.

Despite the Covid restrictions, cricket was alive and well. At its best the Test match remains the pinnacle of the sport, capable of conjuring drama and revealing character in a manner beyond most other sports. The three old(ish) formats of the game were working rather well together. This only served to strengthen the view that the introduction of a gimmicky fourth format in 2021 in England and Wales, involving teams with no genuine support base, was an act of folly.

In the meantime, on the domestic front in the UK, the Bob Willis Trophy – a competition hastily arranged to replace the County Championship in the final six weeks of the 2020 season – was validated by the presence of the two best county sides in the country (Essex and Somerset) reaching a five-day final at Lord's at the end of September (more of which later). No spectators were allowed but it was still possible for members of the public to watch. Even the octogenarian supporters out there discovered the delights of streaming the action – something the counties had undertaken with increasing sophistication.

Against all the odds, the 2020 season had been a minor triumph. Due to the pandemic the game was poorer yet more popular. Despite all the impediments, there was reason to celebrate and to be optimistic about the future. So what follows, which explores some of the charms, the quirks and the peculiar allure of cricket from a variety of perspectives, is not intended as a memorial for long-lost sepia days. The game is still alive. Somehow it survived 2020. With enlightened guardians it can do better than that in the years to come.

But what about that title? Well, surprise, surprise, we haven't been able to match those of Harper Lee, J. D. Salinger or Ken Kesey. In the end we settled upon *Late Cuts*. I've played a few of those in my time, not always with success, as you will discover when I find myself facing Derek Underwood on page 246. I also have to recognize the passage of time and the fact that I am not so actively involved with the game now. The pandemic – even though at the time of writing I've managed to avoid it – has something to do with that. So do the newspapers I have worked for over the last three decades.

Back in 1989 the *Observer* sought me out to be their cricket correspondent; they were offering me considerably more money and a much longer career than Somerset CCC could ever do. So, after a bit of agonizing, I retired from professional cricket at the age of 34 and a few people had the good grace to ask me why, implying they did not necessarily think I was over the hill yet. Having stayed with the *Observer* for thirty-one years, I guess there is no reason to regret that decision.

By 2020 I had been working for the *Guardian* for a dozen years as well, but the pandemic had taken its toll and the group was looking for volunteers for redundancy in the sports department. Once again I was confronted with a hard-to-refuse offer from a newspaper, but this time it involved leaving rather than joining. I'll miss working with sympathetic, civilized employers and colleagues and – who knows? – maybe I'll re-appear in their columns occasionally in the future. But at least – as when leaving Somerset all those years ago – I have been spared listening to someone from above having to initiate an uncomfortable conversation about my future. It seems I have managed to shrewdly go before splitting too many infinitives.

I have enjoyed being the cricket correspondent of the *Observer* and the *Guardian*; these have been great posts to hold and I'm aware they have been occupied by some wonderful correspondents in the past. I guess I'll miss the position as much as the work, and in 2021 I'm sure I'll be pining for the odd bit of press-box banter and the free pass to another

Test match but I will not miss that blank screen miles from home late on a damp Sunday night. And at least there is now no compulsion to watch The Hundred, which I'll try not to mention again in whatever follows here.

1

Selection

'My God, look what they've sent me.'

England captain A. C. MacLaren, 1902

THEY KEPT PICKING him for fifteen years but Ian Botham's description of a Test selector, delivered at a cricket dinner in the 1980s, was none too flattering. 'They bring him out of the loft, take the dust sheet off, give him a pink gin and sit him there. He can't go out of a 30-mile radius of London because he's normally too pissed to get back.'

Well, this would have raised a laugh. In that era the selectors were sometimes old amateurs, who were more likely to be gin-slingers, and – expenses apart – they were unpaid. I'm not sure they were all drunkards, though. In fact, the chairman of selectors when Ian was England captain was Alec Bedser, very much the professional's professional as a player, and he held the post longer than anyone in history – for thirteen seasons.

Ray Illingworth, another old pro, was the first chairman to be paid, partly because he was dovetailing as England's team manager in the mid-1990s. Ever since then it has been a job with a salary, during which time David Graveney, Geoff Miller, James Whitaker and Ed Smith have held the post now known as the national selector. Smith, in particular, was well paid. He certainly could not afford to be seen with a pink gin during working hours. However, idiosyncratic sunglasses were permitted.

The task of a selector is simple: he/she has to deliver teams/ touring squads and then let the coach and captain get on with it. The basics of the job are so straightforward that there are thousands of armchair selectors out there with thousands of different theories who think they can do better. We can all pluck out a dozen names or more and then offer our expert opinion with absolute confidence, in the comforting knowledge that we will seldom be held to account. No one will remember our crackpot theories for long. But it is trickier for the real selectors; their mistakes are remembered far more frequently than any triumphs.

In reality it is very rarely a matter of making brilliant, trailblazing choices that no one else has ever contemplated before. More often it is a case of taking the least bad option as events dictate the next move. Consider England's leading run-scorer, Alastair Cook. He was always going to play Test cricket but his elevation to the team did not come about as the final step of a carefully crafted plan. Rather, in March 2006, he was rushed halfway around the world to Nagpur from the Caribbean, where he was touring with the England A team, after both Marcus Trescothick and Michael Vaughan were suddenly unable to play in the first Test against India. Upon arrival in Nagpur, Cook was catapulted straight into the team; he hit 60 in his first innings and an unbeaten century in his second. There followed 160 more Test matches for Cook without ever being dropped. Yet he needed a couple of sudden absentees to get started.

Successful selection is dependent on solid research, sound judgement, the odd hunch, a bit of luck and a reservoir of decent players. It can be hampered by tunnel vision, a desperation to pursue fairness rather than the best side, inflexibility, prejudice, wishful thinking and a dearth of good players. We remember the bad selections far more easily than the good ones and they are usually more fun to revisit. But let's try to identify some of the good ones first.

In fact the Lancashire captain, A. C. MacLaren, a stately galleon of a cricketer at the start of the twentieth century, will appear in both categories. MacLaren was an amateur, of course, but often an impecunious one, and it may be that he was capable of starting an argument in an empty room. He went to Harrow, where he declared that his fag was 'quite useless' and 'a snotty little bugger', which is a rare description of Winston Churchill.

Neville Cardus hero-worshipped MacLaren, partly because he was the captain of his beloved Lancashire, but perhaps also because Cardus was indebted to him for enhancing his career as a journalist. At the age of 50 MacLaren led a scratch side to victory over the almost invincible Australians of 1921 and Cardus was, of course, there to report it. In fact, having badgered his office to let him cover the match in Eastbourne, it transpired that he was the only leading journalist present to record this staggering defeat of the tourists. This was one of just two games that the Australians lost on their thirty-eight-match tour. Cardus was in clover at Eastbourne, while his peers were elsewhere.

Cardus described his hero as 'the noblest Roman of them all... there never was a cricketer with more than the grandeur of A. C. MacLaren'. Lancashire's autocratic captain was obviously a formidable batsman, capable of scoring runs in isolation and, occasionally, in bulk – he hit 424 not out against Somerset at Taunton in 1895, which became the highest score ever recorded in first-class cricket at the time. Alan Gibson took a slightly different view of him to Cardus (though he might not have expressed it too readily in his presence): 'England may have had worse captains but I would be hard put to name two or three,' he wrote in a wonderful book, *The Cricket Captains of England*, that surveyed England's leaders on the field up to Mike Gatting. However, Gibson acknowledges that MacLaren was box office, though he puts it more elegantly than that; in the twenty-first century we would have made sure that we did not miss any of his press conferences. 'England under MacLaren must have been a good side to watch, save for the partisans, but an uncomfortable side in which to play,' he wrote.

The bald statistics are not in MacLaren's favour. He led England in four Ashes series – in 1899, 1901/02, 1902 and 1909 – and Australia won all of them. Yet MacLaren's selection of S. F. Barnes for the tour of 1901/02 was surely a good one – and Barnes was not necessarily an obvious choice at the time. He was already 28 years of age but had only appeared in seven first-class matches in his life as he preferred to play in league cricket and for his beloved Staffordshire in the Minor Counties competition. In 1901, when a professional in the Lancashire League, Barnes was invited to bowl at MacLaren in the nets at Old Trafford. Cardus recalls the event and quotes MacLaren: 'He thumped me on the left thigh. He hit my gloves from a length. He actually said, "Sorry, sir!" and I said, "Don't be sorry, Barnes. You're coming to Australia with me."'

And so he did. Barnes took seven wickets in his first Test in Sydney and England won the match. But by the third game he was injured through over-bowling and the series was eventually lost 4-1. Nonetheless, selecting Barnes in the first place was assuredly a good decision – just as Javed Miandad thrusting Wasim Akram, who had hardly played any first-class cricket at the time, into the Pakistan Test side in 1985 was soon justified. Of course, both cases look like the most obvious selections imaginable with hindsight since Barnes and Akram proved to be such brilliant, innovative bowlers.

Sydney Barnes was extremely single-minded, stubborn, difficult to handle and always determined to be properly remunerated for his skills. And MacLaren was MacLaren, haughty and intransigent. The relationship was bound to be spiky, to say the least. On the trip home from that Ashes series the boat hit rough seas and MacLaren, never known for his cheery optimism, famously remarked, 'At least if we go down we'll take that bugger Barnes down with us.'

Barnes took 189 wickets in twenty-seven Test matches at 16.43 apiece. No bowler has taken wickets so swiftly or cheaply for England. He was the ultimate craftsman, capable of spinning the ball, not cutting it, as he was always keen to point out, in both directions at medium pace. After his retirement he became a calligrapher. In the 2012 *Wisden* Peter Gibbs – once of Oxford University, Derbyshire and Staffordshire – wrote a lovely piece in which he describes being the youngster in the side given the daunting task of looking after Barnes, now into his nineties, while he was watching Staffordshire playing. Gibbs was asked to get some autographs from Barnes, an undertaking he attempted with some trepidation and a biro. Barnes demanded a fountain pen. 'Giving him a biro was like asking Yehudi Menuhin to play the ukulele,' wrote Gibbs.

A good selection may come in the form of omitting someone surprising. Alec Bedser might be the nearest any England bowler has come to Barnes. He cut the ball, rather than spinning it, as well as propelling inswingers for which Godfrey Evans often stood up at the stumps. After the Second World War Bedser carried the England bowling tirelessly with modest support, the ball shrinking into his massive hands for over after over. I once disappointed my wife when looking at Michelangelo's *David* in Florence by observing 'Blimey, he's got hands like Alec Bedser.'

Eventually some assistance for Bedser was at hand in the form of Brian Statham, Fred Trueman and Frank Tyson. As ever, the first Test of the 1954/55 Ashes series was in Brisbane, a venue that has prompted some odd decisions by England captains. In recent times, if 2002 still counts, Nasser Hussain inserted Australia, who were 364-2 at the close of play on the first day. The match was lost by 384 runs. Hussain was lambasted for his decision but he found himself in good company.

In 1954 Len Hutton, having omitted all his spinners – and he had some good ones available in Johnny Wardle and Bob Appleyard – put Australia in at the Gabba. They made 601-8 and won the match by an innings and 154 runs. Bedser, who had been recovering from shingles, took 1-131 from 37 overs and witnessed as many as seven catches go down off his bowling. Neither Statham nor Tyson were any more effective.

Three weeks later England were in Sydney for the second Test and Hutton, after much agonizing, made a momentous decision, 'the most painful of my career,' he wrote later. 'I realize now I should have handled such a delicate matter differently.' He dropped Bedser, the backbone of the England side for so long. He picked both spinners but the critical difference was that something clicked for Tyson, who had by now moved to a shorter run-up. In Sydney, Tyson shredded the Australian batting line-up through magnificent, unadulterated speed and the pattern was set for the series.

Hutton, England's first professional captain, had made the right decision, albeit in the wrong way. After all Hutton's deliberating, Bedser only learned of his omission when looking at the team sheet pinned up in the dressing room half an hour before the start of play. The strategy was rather better than the man-management in an era when the captain had to do everything himself. England, with Tyson running riot, won the series 3-1. Bedser played just one more Test match against South Africa in the summer of 1955.

In 1956 England obviously decided that the touring Australian batsmen would be fragile on turning pitches especially against the spinners, Jim Laker and Tony Lock. But England's batting was none too sturdy either. The first Test at Nottingham, a wet one, was drawn. Australia won the second at Lord's by 185 runs. The selection panel – chaired by Gubby Allen and including Les Ames, Wilf Wooller and Cyril Washbrook – was by now very concerned about England's batting line-up. As they were mulling over the team for the third Test at Leeds, Allen instructed Washbrook to go and get some beer. By the time he returned, his fellow selectors had chosen him for the next match. Washbrook, once the regular opening partner of Hutton and the first professional captain of Lancashire, was 41 and he had not played Test cricket since the 1950/51 tour of Australia. 'Surely the situation isn't as desperate as that,' he said. Beyond the portals of Lord's there was consternation and despair that the selectors had chosen one of their own committee.

A few days later at Headingley Peter May won a good toss since the pitch was expected to assist the spinners, but England were soon 17-3. May was still at the crease and he recalled afterwards, 'I have never felt so glad in my life as when I saw who was coming in.' It was Washbrook. This pair shared a partnership of 187, May making 101 and Washbrook 98 before being lbw to Richie Benaud. England's total of 325 was enough to ensure an innings victory as Laker and Lock set to work on a deteriorating surface. Now the press and the public hailed a masterstroke. Washbrook failed to reach double figures in his two other innings in the series, but the tide had been turned. After Laker's 19 wickets in the next match at Old Trafford and a soggy draw at The Oval,

England won the series 2-1. The recall of Washbrook had not been such a bad idea after all.

Of course, anyone can select the exceptional players. It would not have taken too much insight to see that David Gower, Mike Atherton, Ian Bell or Mark Ramprakash were high-quality batsmen destined for Test cricket (even though the latter provides a reminder that nothing is guaranteed once you get there). So the unlikely selections that come good are a better indication of the fertile, lateral thinking that leads to the odd inspired selection. In the modern era, which encompasses players I have played against or watched, Tony Greig and his selection panel (Ken Barrington, Len Hutton and the former umpire Charlie Elliott, along with Bedser) produced one of those.

In July 1975 Geoffrey Boycott was in self-imposed exile; Mike Denness had just been sacked by Bedser as England captain after a massive defeat in the first Test against Australia at Edgbaston, a decision the outgoing captain agreed with, which is an unusual state of affairs. In a letter to Bedser a few weeks afterwards, Denness wrote 'the decision you came to in the end was undoubtedly for the better and the interest of the game... I only regret that you personally had to take so much stick from the "mass media".' So Greig took over as captain and, in the absence of Boycott, he decided he needed some no-nonsense bloody-mindedness to blunt the pace and aggression of Dennis Lillee and Jeff Thomson, who had so tormented Denness and the other England batsmen during the previous winter's tour. In Australia Denness's form hit rock bottom to the extent that Doug Walters in the gully would complain – just loudly enough – to the slip cordon as the England captain made his way to the crease: 'Oh no! Look who's coming in now. We're going to be held up for at least another ten minutes.'

After Denness had been sacked, the new captain consulted widely around the county circuit. According to the man finally selected, David Steele, 'Greigy went to see the umpires and they gave him a nod. Good move, that.' Steele – at the age of 33 with a first-class batting average of 31 for unfashionable Northamptonshire, prematurely grey hair and a pair of National Health spectacles (or so it seemed) – was pitchforked into the Test team. At Lord's before the match, Hutton greeted him as 'Dennis' but Steele was not too bothered by that. He was going out to bat for England.

This was in the pre-helmet age and out strode Steele at number three on his debut, looking like a jockey from the shoulders up because the peak of his cap was pointing skywards. Actually it took rather a long time for him to get to the middle because, having left the unfamiliar home dressing room, he took one flight of stairs too many and ended up in the toilets on the lower-ground floor of the Lord's Pavilion before backtracking. Upon arrival in the middle, he was greeted by Lillee as 'Groucho'.

Clive Taylor of *The Sun* memorably dubbed him 'the bank clerk who went to war'. Hooking Lillee three times off the front foot – he was always on the front foot – Steele hit a half-century and added 96 with captain Greig. He topped the England batting averages after three Tests, hitting 365 runs at 60.83. There was no winter tour, which meant he was free to attend the BBC's *Sports Personality of the Year* programme. And he won the trophy. At the time he was only the second cricketer, after Jim Laker, to do so. He also won 1756 lamb chops from a local butcher, which was the number of runs he scored in his benefit year. It is not beyond the realms of possibility that he counted them all.

The following summer Steele played in all five Tests against the all-conquering, non-grovelling West Indies, having hit a century in the first match at Trent Bridge. Along with just four other England cricketers, he survived to play the entire series. But he was surplus to requirements for the winter tour to India and the reason given by Greig was that Steele's method would not be suited to the trial by spin that awaited England there. Steele felt hard done by after being on the receiving end of some serious pace bowling in his eight Test matches and he may have had a point. I'm not so sure he was that weak against spin, although this is based on slightly dubious evidence: the recollection that he usually played me all right. The challenge from Bedi, Chandrasekhar and Prasanna might have been slightly different. Steele was quick to plunge on to the front foot, which you are not supposed to do against spinners, and he could look limited and cumbersome but he certainly had the calm single-mindedness to be successful and in those eight Tests he proved beyond doubt how he relished playing at the highest level.

So that was it for Steele as an England cricketer, though he kept playing county cricket until 1984. He was also a handy left-arm spinner, who once should have had Viv Richards stumped by a mile when bowling for Derbyshire against Somerset. His exasperation was obvious; soon after his escape, Viv hit one of his innocent deliveries into a distant tree, which prompted Steele to chide the great man, 'Look, you're not supposed to knock conkers down until September.' He was a very good selection in 1975 and a memorable one, who captured the hearts of the cricketing public and beyond.

Another unlikely England Test cricketer, who also began his career with Northamptonshire, was Neil Mallender. By the time he was called up at the age of 30 he had been at Somerset for almost five years. He was chosen for the Leeds Test of 1992 as a Headingley specialist plucked out to bowl on what was the most capricious surface in the country. This is no longer the case, but in the 1980s and 1990s the ball would dart off the pitch malevolently whenever the clouds rolled in over Leeds. Accuracy and an ability to hit the seam were more important than pace, which the opposition, Pakistan, possessed in abundance with Waqar Younis and Wasim Akram always threatening with the new ball and utterly devastating with the old one.

England arrived at Headingley one down in what was a fiery series. Ian Botham had just played his last Test match at Lord's, David Gower had been recalled, Graham Gooch was the captain and Mallender was the new boy. I had been in the same dressing room as Neil during my last three seasons at Somerset and had come to admire him. He was a dedicated cricketer with a big heart and massive feet. He did not bowl at express pace but was lively enough to pose a constant threat at county level. At his best he hit the seam and a good length more often than most. He might have chosen Headingley as the place to make his debut. The wicket obviously suited him there and he was also born in Yorkshire, at Kirk Sandall near Doncaster.

I knew Neil's routine well from the county circuit and this included having a beer or two on the eve of a big match – for relaxation purposes. I was concerned that he might desert this routine, having being elevated to the giddy heights of the England side, and that he might suffer a debilitating restless night as a consequence. By now I was working for the *Observer* and for this game I had also been enlisted by *Test Match Special*. I was staying in the same hotel as the England team, just north of Leeds, and felt it my patriotic duty – as well as my pleasure – to seek him out for a beer or two on the Wednesday night. It seemed vital that Neil, who did not need much persuasion, should stick to his routine to ensure that he was as relaxed as possible on his England debut (and it was just a beer or two).

The following morning England were in the field and I was in the tiny *TMS* commentary box at Leeds that was perched right behind the bowler's arm at the Rugby Stand end. Mallender's moment had arrived at Headingley and so had Fred Trueman, who was on air at the start of play. It soon became apparent that Fred had never seen Mallender bowl before and he was aghast at what he saw (Mallender had quite a plodding, mechanical approach to the wicket). 'England bowler? England bowler?' he spluttered, shaking his head in despair. 'You must be having me on.' (Fred was never in the best of moods at his old home ground as a few deep scars were inevitably reopened even before he had reached the commentary box.) Fred was not aware of Mallender's Yorkshire roots, though that may not have made any difference to his initial reaction. He did not pull his punches. To summarize: Fred, having watched an over or two, was adamant that Mallender was most definitely not worthy of taking the new ball for England on a pitch that *Wisden* said 'lived up to every word of its wicked reputation'. Once Fred had passed on the microphone in despair, Mallender immediately took two wickets in quick succession and his nerves settled; he ended with three in the innings as Pakistan were bowled out for 197.

Graham Gooch then hit one of his Headingley hundreds, with solid support from Mike Atherton, to give England a lead of 123. It should have been much bigger but some brilliant reverse-swing bowling by Waqar prompted England to collapse from 292-2 to 320 all out. Mallender was in rhythm right from the start in the second innings and finished with 5-50 from 23 overs. England won by six wickets and the series was level ahead of the final Test at The Oval.

Mallender was selected for that one as well and bowled respectably enough in less helpful conditions as England lost the match by ten wickets. He never appeared in Test cricket again except as an umpire in three matches in the winter of 2003/04. The peripatetic existence of an international umpire was not for him but he remains on the first-class list and is much respected there. And he always has the memory of Headingley. For one match at least he had been an excellent pick.

Less surprising than Mallender's selection was the elevation of Michael Vaughan and Marcus Trescothick in 1999 and 2000 respectively. Yet it is worth noting that neither of these batsmen, who would become captain and vice-captain in one of England's best ever sides, had particularly good records when they were first picked. A touch of class? Yes. A stack of runs? No.

Vaughan was plucked out specifically for the tour of South Africa, Duncan Fletcher's first undertaking as England's coach. Fletcher's influence was more significant in the selection of Trescothick, who needed an injury to Nick Knight to propel him into the England side the following year. Fletcher, as coach of Glamorgan, had witnessed Trescothick hitting 167 on a fast wicket at Taunton in the summer of 1999. Trescothick kept pulling rapid deliveries from Jacques Kallis in front of square and into the stands and he was the only batsman in the match to score more than 50. Fletcher's mind was made up – and once that happened it never changed.

Fletcher once watched David Sales, a prolific, talented batsman for Northamptonshire, in the field; he was at slip while a perspiring Devon Malcolm, who was in the middle of a long spell, was at deep backward square leg. The ball trickled fine on the leg side towards the boundary. Malcolm from a distance hurtled after it; Sales, who probably had less far to run, did not move a muscle at slip. Fletcher never forgot that – he spied laziness and Sales never got his chance. By the same token, we can surmise that Graeme Swann would never have played for England if Fletcher had stayed in his post for another few years. Swann was on Fletcher's first tour to South Africa in 1999 as a precocious, wise-cracking 20-year-old and he did not impress the new coach. He was written off by Fletcher and so he had to wait for another nine years and the advent of Peter Moores as coach to play Test cricket – a delay that was not a complete disaster for him as by then Swann knew his game.

Winning sides generally prompt the odd plaudit for the selectors. By the skin of their teeth the selectors managed to keep Bob Willis in their side for the Headingley Test of 1981. It was only after the letter inviting Mike Hendrick to play in the match was intercepted in the offices of Derbyshire CCC that Willis had been added to the squad, having pleaded with Alec Bedser that he was fit enough to play. Even then, Mike Brearley was castigating himself after two grim days back in charge on the grounds that he had not selected John Emburey for the Headingley match – maybe instead of Willis, who took 8-43 on the final day.

In the summer of 2005 there was the greatest ever Ashes series (at least for those residing in the northern hemisphere) and that encompassed at least two excellent selections for the England side. Kevin Pietersen made his debut in the first Test of the series at Lord's. Now he seems the obvious choice but at the time it was a close-run thing between Pietersen and Graham Thorpe, who had reached veteran status after playing 100 Tests for England. Fletcher and his selectors, who rarely disagreed with him, went for the burgeoning talent and the evidence of their eyes rather than Thorpe's impressive record – and, of course, they were right.

The other triumph was the presence of Simon Jones in that series. He would only play eighteen Tests because of injury woes. There were two matches in 2002, the second of which saw him tear his knee ligaments as he dived in the outfield in Brisbane, and sixteen games in 2004 and 2005. Fletcher spotted his potential; Jones possessed pace and the ability to reverse-swing the ball but, unusually, he learned how to bowl effectively while playing for England rather than before he was selected.

In 2005 it was Jones with his ability to deliver reverse swing that spooked the Australian batsmen as much as anything else. His record is remarkable, especially when compared with that of Graham Dilley twenty years earlier. Jones enjoyed victory in eleven of his eighteen Tests; four were drawn and just three lost (and in that Brisbane Test defeat he was unable to participate after his injury on the first morning). Dilley, who had a highly respectable record thanks to his ability to swing the ball at pace, played forty-one Tests for England, taking 138 wickets, yet he experienced victory just twice (at Headingley in 1981 and Brisbane in 1986). Jones (59 wickets in those eighteen Tests) may have made a greater impression and he certainly enjoyed more success, though even he cannot match the impact of another pace bowler from an epic Ashes series in 1954/55: Frank Tyson, who took 76 wickets from his seventeen matches. However, Jones was another excellent pick and not necessarily an obvious one.

More recently there have been a few others that look obvious choices – but only with the passage of time. When England needed another batsman for the decisive final Test of the 2009 Ashes at The Oval, there was a bit of panic and much tub-thumping in the media: this was a national emergency; the selectors should persuade Marcus Trescothick out of retirement for one match or perhaps they should recall Mark Ramprakash, who was still scoring prolifically on the county circuit for Surrey. Instead the selectors stayed calm and stuck to the existing pecking order, which meant that Jonathan Trott was picked for the first time in Test cricket. He repaid that faith with 41 and 119 in the final Test of the summer and the Ashes were secured.

Yet, ahead of the T20 World Cup in the West Indies in 2010, Andy Flower and his fellow selectors deserted the established pecking order and plucked out a fresh opening pair from nowhere in the shape of Michael Lumb and Craig Kieswetter. This pair had excelled in practice matches, casting aside any inhibitions when playing for the Lions against the senior side in Dubai, and those in charge decided to take a remarkable punt just before the tournament. Kieswetter, hitting his first international half-century, was man of the match in the final against Australia. A neat selection.

Even Joe Root's first Test appearance took everyone by surprise in December 2012. England had just won two matches in a row in India, at Mumbai and Kolkata; the assumption was that they would therefore keep the same side for the final match in Nagpur, where a draw was sufficient to secure the series. But captain Alastair Cook had seen something in the nets that really made an impression. It was the ease with which Root played the spinners with the soft hands of a veteran that convinced Cook to change his line-up. Root was selected instead of Samit Patel, which really does seem an obvious move now. On his debut Root delivered a patient 73 in his first innings before giving his first whispered press conference as an England player plus an unbeaten 20 in the second.

In 2014 England selected Moeen Ali for the first time. That seemed to make some sense since his ability with the bat had long been admired. But they picked him primarily as a frontline spinner, a role that he had never had with Worcestershire. After 61 Tests, Moeen had taken 189 wickets; of English spinners, only Derek Underwood, Graeme Swann and Jim Laker have taken more. That was clever. So too was the decision to go with Jofra Archer for the 2019 World Cup. As with Pietersen in 2005, the selectors had the wit to trust their eyes rather than the old hierarchy.

A fundamental in good selection is that there should be mutual respect between the chief selector and the captain, which brings us back to A. C. MacLaren and a relationship that did not work so well. Lord Hawke, the captain of Yorkshire, was the chairman of selectors in 1902, who once delivered the imprecation 'Pray God no professional may ever captain England.' Well, he had a bit of bother with MacLaren that summer, his amateur captain from across the Pennines. The two autocrats were locked in conflict throughout the series. We have now moved on to selectorial calamities.

Rain saved Australia in the first match of that famous summer at Edgbaston and it ruined the second Test at Lord's. Before the only Test match ever played in Sheffield, Hawke selected Bill Lockwood and Schofield Haigh as fast bowlers. MacLaren decided he wanted Barnes (again) and a few hours before the game he sent a telegram to summon him to Bramall Lane. Barnes duly arrived and played in the match, taking seven wickets while both Lockwood and Haigh were omitted. Lord Hawke was none too pleased. Australia won the Test by 143 runs to take a 1-0 lead in the series.

This was just the start of the selectorial shenanigans. For the next match in Manchester, Hawke took the precaution of picking just eleven players to ensure that MacLaren would have to lead out the team that the selectors wanted, but in the end he decided to add one reserve, Fred Tate of Sussex, confident that not even MacLaren would pick him. 'My God, look what they've sent me,' was MacLaren's reported reaction to the team he was given. It is a phrase that cricket correspondents have since rushed towards whenever they smell divisions between the selectors and the captain. We can be sure that MacLaren was furious at Old Trafford and this fury led him to play Tate instead of the most reliable all-rounder in the country, the Yorkshireman George Hirst.

What followed was a gripping struggle that became known as 'Tate's match', a rare instance of a game being identified by the nightmarish struggles of one of its participants. It would have been kinder to call it 'Trumper's match' (England were 'unable to keep Victor quiet before lunch' – not a phrase I heard frequently in my career – and Trumper cracked 104 in 115 minutes) or 'Trumble's match' (the Australian, Hugh Trumble, took ten wickets in the game). Australia won by three runs. Tate took 2-7 in Australia's second innings but hardly anyone outside the Tate family ever remembers that. They do remember that he dropped a crucial catch on the boundary that allowed Joe Darling to top-score in that innings and that he came to the wicket at number eleven with eight needed for England to win the match. He edged a four and was bowled three balls later. Tate never played another Test although his son, Maurice, would be the mainstay of England's bowling two decades later. Fred deserves our sympathy but the evidence suggests he was not a good selection. That wasn't his fault.

Nor does the selection of Otto Nothling look that good, although this conclusion – like many others – depends heavily upon hindsight. Brought up in Brisbane, Nothling was a medic who went on to study at Sydney University. He was also a fine, exuberant all-round sportsman who would play nineteen games at full-back for Australia's rugby union side. In December 1928 he played his one Test match for Australia as an energetic all-rounder who bowled with the new ball and batted at number seven. In the match, which was won by England by eight wickets, he bowled 46 economical overs – without taking a wicket – as well as scoring 8 and 44. Not the worst debut. So why do we single him out? Because he is the only man to be preferred in the Australian side to Don Bradman in Test cricket.

Bradman had played in the previous Test in Brisbane, which was his debut. He batted at number seven in his first innings and made one run, to be followed by 18 in the second as Australia were defeated by 675 runs. Bradman was dropped and Nothling took his place for the game in Sydney. For the next match in Melbourne Bradman was recalled and hit 79 and 112 – though England still won by three wickets. He was never dropped again.

For this winter only Walter Hammond remained the greatest batsman in the world, an accolade that would belong to

Bradman for the next decade. It may be unfair to focus on Nothling, who cheerfully dined out on his fate for many years afterwards. The selectors did not necessarily err by picking him, but we can probably conclude that they did make a mistake when dropping Bradman.

Nothling's selection and his subsequent omission is an oddity; the omission and subsequent selection of Basil D'Oliveira in 1968 was a scandal. The saga is well known and has inevitably prompted much speculation, most notably in Peter Oborne's riveting book, *Basil D'Oliveira: Cricket and Conspiracy: The Untold Story*, which outlines his view that Tory grandees and the cricketing establishment – including the captain, Colin Cowdrey – conspired to keep D'Oliveira out of the tour party originally selected for the tour of South Africa in 1968/69. Then after a great furore they summoned him up as a replacement for Tom Cartwright, who had declared that he was not fit enough to travel. This prompted President Vorster of South Africa to cancel the tour. In the space of a few weeks the MCC selectors had contrived to outrage the liberals in England and the proponents of apartheid in South Africa, probably a unique achievement.

Mike Brearley in his recent book, *On Cricket*, outlined how he was told by a third party that Doug Insole – a central figure since he was the chairman of selectors at the time – had eventually confided at a carol service in 2016 that the original decision of the selectors, which was to pick D'Oliveira, 'had been reversed'. Insole, who died in 2017, had been great friends with Brearley, having managed a triumphant England tour of Australia with him in the winter of 1978/79, and he had always denied any conspiracy theories – even to Brearley – while remaining tight-lipped about one of cricket's greatest dramas. Nor did it help future historians that the minutes of that notorious selection meeting at Lord's mysteriously went missing. Or maybe that isn't so mysterious. I'm still awaiting the film.

Brearley writes on Insole's refusal to reveal all: 'He put his sense of duty and confidentiality ahead of self-justification.' It is hard to avoid the conclusion that the selectors were leaned upon, though at least two of them, Alec Bedser and Peter May, were known to be keen to maintain ties with South Africa – and that would have been the case with some of the non-selectors, MCC grandees attending the meeting in a crowded committee room. But we will never know exactly what happened now. What is absolutely certain is that the D'Oliveira affair displayed selectorial cock-ups on a monumental scale. No one emerged with any credit from this saga – except D'Oliveira.

May withdrew as a selector in 1968 soon after this fiasco, returning in 1982 when he was appointed chairman of the panel. His final season in charge was 1988 and that did not go frightfully well either. England were playing the West Indies and it was the year of the four captains and a lot of different England cricketers. I was the thirty-fourth player to be picked for England that summer when, out of the blue, I was invited to play against Sri Lanka in an ODI right at the end of the season, a statistic I do not boast about much.

The Test captains were Mike Gatting (ostensibly dropped after alleged misdemeanours on the rest day of the first

Test in Nottingham), John Emburey (he was not taking any wickets), Chris Cowdrey and Graham Gooch. Of those selections, that of Cowdrey for the Headingley Test was the most eye-catching and the most controversial. It was misguided to pick him in the first place and yet unfair to dispose of him so quickly. Before the Headingley Test they had enquired about Gooch's availability to captain the team via Insole, who could act as an intermediary at Essex; Gooch explained that he had already signed to play for Western Province that winter, which meant he was not available for the winter tour to India, so the selectors decided not to pursue that option. There were other contenders from outside the team, like Kim Barnett and Mark Nicholas, but perhaps Cowdrey's experience of Test cricket in the winter of 1984/85 in India helped him, so too the fact that his Kent side were leading the Championship at the time despite losing their first three games of the season. Less relevant, though this undoubtedly added spice to the story, was the fact that Cowdrey was Peter May's godson.

At their first meeting Cowdrey was told by May that he was earmarked to take the side to India in the winter and then his godfather confided there was little or no expectation that England would be able to defeat the West Indies in either of the two remaining Tests. Cowdrey was also told he could not pick Paul Downton and David Gower, his two best friends in the game, though under protest May relented and allowed him to select one of them. So Cowdrey opted for Gower.

The match at Headingley was lost by ten wickets, Cowdrey scoring 0 and 5. Before the Oval Test Cowdrey had met with the selectors and this time he had to agree to the dropping of Gower; he returned to Canterbury for a match against Somerset and in his first innings he was hit on the foot by a yorker from fast bowler Adrian Jones. An X-ray determined there was no fracture but there was a nasty bruise. Upon hearing this news, May was soon on the phone and Cowdrey gained the distinct impression that this blow to the foot now provided an excuse for the Cowdrey experiment to be ditched immediately. 'Could you play in two hours' time?' Cowdrey was asked. 'Obviously not,' was the answer. So the selectors quickly went back to Gooch, who was by now more amenable to the idea of captaining England. Already the notion of Cowdrey captaining the side in India had been jettisoned, though he was never properly informed of this. In fact, that tour never took place as India refused to accept the presence of England players with strong South African connections (like Gooch).

That match at Headingley must have seemed like a disaster for Cowdrey at the time, but before long he contrived, quite brilliantly, to have it as the centrepiece of many of his speeches, his relationship with May merely adding to his arsenal of potent – and hilarious – ammunition. At the end of the season May was replaced as chairman by Ted Dexter, whose period in charge produced a few other selectorial decisions that prompted some head-scratching.

The tour to India in 1992/93 did not quite go according to plan either. Gooch was still the captain and they took the decision to omit David Gower again, who no longer fitted into the Gooch/Micky Stewart ethos and was in the autumn of his career. Even so, this was a provocative act and, to some, a cowardly one. Gower had performed well in his comeback in 1992 and his touch of class – allied to his experience – might have been invaluable in India. But they could not be bothered to try to incorporate a gentle maverick in their squad. Gooch later acknowledged this was a mistake. Jack Russell was also omitted. Instead they chose Dermot Reeve and the Yorkshire keeper, Richard Blakey. These selections – especially the omission of Gower – prompted a special general meeting of MCC members, which demanded a vote of no confidence in the England selectors; this was rejected by 6135 votes to 4600 as the postal voters overturned the majority in the hall. That majority may well have been right. Gower could exasperate but he had always made himself available for England, unlike the senior players selected for the India trip who had been quite prepared to play in South Africa on rebel tours rather than stick with the national side – this was the case with Gooch, Mike Gatting and John Emburey (twice).

The tour was a shambles and this was epitomized by the selection in Calcutta. Thirty-six hours before the start of the first Test match India named their eleven, which contained three spinners. England's think tank – comprising Gooch, coach Keith Fletcher, Alec Stewart and Gatting – noted this and picked four seamers plus the leg-spinner Ian Salisbury, who had not been an original selection for the tour and had only been flown out to bowl in the nets and to gain a bit of experience.

Emburey and Phil Tufnell were left on the sidelines, in part because Navjot Sidhu, India's opening batsman, kept hitting Emburey for six in two warm-up games. Emburey apparently talked himself out of playing. So the pace attack consisted of Devon Malcolm, Paul Jarvis, Chris Lewis and the left-armer Paul Taylor, who had to be used sparingly since his footmarks created some lovely rough for the Indian off-spinner Rajesh Chauhan. England's most successful bowler was the part-time off-spinner Graeme Hick, who took 5-28 in the match. Mohammad Azharuddin, a captain who had been under extreme pressure after a sequence of poor results, hit 182 and India won the first Test of the series by eight wickets. It did not get any better for England after that.

In this century tunnel vision has too often taken over. There has been no shortage of conscientious agonizing among the selectors but there has also been an inability to see the wider picture. Darren Pattinson was by no means the worst bowler ever to play for England but he might have been the most astonished to do so. He had been planning to go to Alton Towers with his family during the Headingley Test of 2008 against South Africa, but soon Michael Vaughan was leading him out onto the field with the full approval of chief selector Geoff Miller and coach Peter Moores after Ryan Sidebottom had to withdraw at the eleventh hour with a back injury caused by 'sleeping on an uncomfortable mattress'.

Pattinson – the brother of the Aussie paceman James Pattinson – was technically eligible to play for England since he was born in Grimsby even though his mystified father declared, 'He's Australian.' Chris Tremlett was already in the squad but he was overlooked, Matthew Hoggard was at the ground and both Simon Jones and Steve Harmison were still playing with some success for their counties. Pattinson,

though 28 years of age, had only played eleven first-class
matches, six for Nottinghamshire and five for Victoria.
He did not bowl badly at Headingley (2-96 from 30 overs)
but his selection betrayed chaos in the camp; it certainly
drew attention away from Andrew Flintoff's recall after an
eighteen-month absence.

Ian Botham in the commentary box described Pattinson's
call-up as 'the most illogical, pathetic and diabolical piece
of selecting I've ever seen,' and no one seemed to be accus-
ing him of hyperbole. After the match, which England lost
by ten wickets, Vaughan said the selection was 'confused'
and that the team lacked 'togetherness', which prompted
Miller to remind him that the selectors decide the make-up
of the squad, then the captain and the coach choose the final
eleven. After one more Test and another defeat at Edgbaston,
Vaughan suddenly retired as captain after five mostly glorious
years in charge.

There followed a decision resulting from even greater tunnel
vision, which would have more long-lasting consequences.
England now needed a new captain and, to my amazement,
they appointed Kevin Pietersen. I might argue with those who
call me work-shy but it is true that I very seldom rang the
Guardian's sports desk to insist that there was a column that
I simply had to write. Yet, on hearing the news of Pietersen's
appointment, that's what I did and it began on the theme of
tunnel vision.

Hugh Morris, the cricket director, Geoff Miller and Peter
Moores, who had never had a fruitful relationship with
Pietersen, persuaded themselves that they needed a captain

who could take control in all three formats; this was their fatal error. By doing that there were barely any candidates left and the most obvious one was suddenly Pietersen. Often we sensitive writers complain about the headlines given to our pieces but on this occasion I could not quibble with 'Strauss, not Pietersen, should be leading England'. This was not an anti-Pietersen stance; it was an anti-stupidity stance. I admired Pietersen the cricketer hugely; in fact, in the previous two years I had found myself defending him more often than most from the usual criticisms. He was a bad choice because he had no experience whatsoever; there was no evidence that he was suited to the job; he was England's best batsman and we were jeopardizing our match-winner. Moreover, there was no suggestion that Pietersen was hungry for the job. The yearning to be captain may well have been a factor when the selectors appointed Ian Botham and Andrew Flintoff in the past and therefore in those two instances there was an element of 'how hard will it be to handle him if he isn't captain?' But there was no suggestion that Pietersen was angling for the post. The bleeding obvious sometimes has merit and in this case Strauss represented the bleeding obvious even if he was to be made the captain in just one or two formats.

Of course, Pietersen won his first Test in charge at The Oval against South Africa by five wickets after scoring a hundred from 137 balls in the first innings. I'm pleased to say this did not change my mind, though it no doubt gave me food for thought. In the end he lasted for six months, which encompassed the Stanford fiasco (not his fault), an unsuccessful ODI series in India and then two more Test matches after a fraught return to the country after the Mumbai bombings.

In his autobiography Pietersen says, 'I bang myself against a brick wall sometimes and ask myself why I ever accepted the England captaincy.' But who would reject such an offer? He says, 'I shouldn't have been captain. Tactically I was fine... but the ECB was a different world.' It all fell apart when Pietersen wanted the coach Peter Moores replaced, a move that had the support of several of the England players. Pietersen described Moores as a decent man but a 'woodpecker', who never gave the players any peace or freedom. In the end the ECB decided to sack both Moores and Pietersen (though the latter then opted to resign). This nurtured the seeds of distrust between Pietersen and his employers and coaches over the next four years. It is just possible that the second part of Pietersen's career might have panned out differently without this episode. We might have been saved an awful bucket of vitriol. In time Moores was, amazingly, invited back (before being sacked again) but there were no second invitations for Pietersen in a leadership role.

Selectors can all too easily succumb to wishful thinking and very often this applies when contemplating English leg-spinners. Even those selectors hitherto regarded as pragmatists go dizzy at the prospect of someone who flicks the ball out of the back of the hand. Ian Salisbury was a substantial wicket-taker at county level; he took five wickets in his first Test against Pakistan at Lord's in 1992, comfortably his best return at that level. In fourteen more Tests spread over eight years he had fifteen more victims so that his wickets ended up costing more than 76 apiece.

The Lancastrian wrist-spinner, Chris Schofield, was in the first batch of cricketers to receive a central contract in 1999, although he ended up playing just two Tests, and not bowling a ball in the first. Mason Crane was selected for the 2017/18 Ashes tour on a wing and a prayer; he played one Test, taking 1-193 and is only just recovering from the experience. Comfortably England's best wrist-spinner for at least half a century is Adil Rashid and his Test figures are not compelling: 60 wickets from nineteen matches at just under 40 apiece. Strangely, in this era the effectiveness of wrist-spinners increases as the length of the game diminishes. No top T20 side can prosper without one, it seems. But Test teams can.

However, wishful thinking can be hard to avoid. Anyone who has attended a selection meeting is susceptible and that includes Ian Botham, who enabled Roy Sully to play one game for Somerset in 1985. There was a mini injury crisis in May ahead of a Sunday League match against Glamorgan. We all turned up and learned of our captain's plan. Sully was 34, a fine club cricketer in Taunton, a bustling all-rounder and a drinking partner of Ian's. Simon Wilde in his excellent biography of Botham reminds me of the pre-match discussion and he quotes Peter Roebuck: 'It was one of the few times where he [Botham] asked us what we thought. Vic Marks and Brian Rose were sceptical. I commented that the lunatics had taken over the asylum.'

The omens were not favourable when Roebuck spotted Sully on the physio's couch before the game started. Sully scored two and was later called upon to bowl some of his medium-pacers. He pulled a hamstring almost immediately but was determined to finish his second over, albeit off a couple of paces. This resulted in two no-balls, after which he limped off the field with figures of 0-15 from two overs. Somerset lost by two wickets. Ian believed in his mates; out of loyalty he might genuinely think they were better than they were, though I'm not sure he had seen Sully play that often. Here was a reminder that the 'startled rabbit plucked out of a hat' policy very rarely works. Yet it did for Australia at the end of the Ashes series of 1986/87. At least, we think it did. No one is quite sure.

Australia were two down in the series ahead of the final Test in Sydney; Allan Border looked to be on his last legs as the Test captain, a job he seemed to do out of duty rather than any deep-seated ambition. In January 1987 Peter Taylor, an orthodox off-spinner aged 30, was worried he might lose his place in the New South Wales side. A few days later he received a phone call from his brother-in-law, an early-rising farmer who had heard the first news bulletin of the day: 'You're in. You've been picked by Australia.' The initial assumption by one and all was that there had been a clerical error; they must have meant Mark Taylor, the highly regarded New South Wales opening batsman, who had been scoring stacks of runs in state cricket. (In fact, Mark would go on to play 104 Tests and to captain an Australian side that was the best in the world.) The off-spinner Taylor was immediately dubbed 'Peter Who' and many years later he was still not sure whether his initial selection was a mistake. Certainly no one was inclined to admit this after that Sydney Test. Taylor was the man of the match. He took 6-76 in the first innings, two more wickets in the second as well as scoring a vital 42 in his second knock as Australia won a tight game by 55 runs.

Border remained as Australia's Test captain after that victory while Taylor would go on to play twelve more Tests and eighty-three ODIs. After a torrid series for the Australians, the wisdom of their selectors was finally heralded. Naturally, I hope Taylor's selection was a mistake.

2

Captains

'What do they expect me to do? Walk around in a
T-shirt with "I'm in charge" on it?'

David Gower (who was soon unable to resist acquiring said
T-shirt before handing it over to Mike Gatting), 1986

TO BE CAPTAIN is the most demanding role in cricket and the
most treacherous. When it all goes wrong the captain is the
obvious man to blame. He has picked the wrong team, he
shouted heads rather than tails, and even if he did manage to
call correctly he subsequently made the wrong decision. The
bowlers were on at the wrong end in the wrong order and
why was there no third slip – or third man? He has lost the
match; soon he is deemed to have lost the dressing room and,
to make matters worse, he's not scoring any runs or taking any
wickets. And he is useless with the media. Everyone is talking
about him behind his back. No wonder an exasperated Derek
Underwood once asked a very sensible question: 'Why does
anybody want to be captain?'

There is a flip side. Being captain can also be the most rewarding job in the game; he can be the puppeteer who has the strings of the players of both sides at his fingertips for as long as five days at a time. He dictates what happens. He plans, he motivates, he wins. A letter to the *Guardian* towards the end of England's 1981 series against Australia highlighted the impact of a captain on a sublime roll: 'On Friday I watched J. M. Brearley directing the fieldsmen very carefully. He then looked up at the sun and made a gesture which suggested that it should move a little squarer. Who is this man?'

Despite Underwood's reservations, most of us think we would like to be captain and that we would be rather good at it even though his duties are never-ending. The captain must be a diplomat, a press officer, a strategist, a confidant and a disciplinarian and he has to contribute runs/wickets as well. There is no respite. Lower down the line at club or village level, it is often his phone that rings on Saturday morning when his opening bowler's eldest has developed chickenpox overnight while his wife is attending an Open University course in Brighton.

Yet there are those moments when everything clicks against the odds and it is all worthwhile. Brearley must have experienced this more often than most, especially when captaining England in that 1981 series; stealing a victory is a wonderful feeling, but stealing two in a row is even better. Richie Benaud must have felt something similar in 1961 when England were racing towards a memorable win at Old Trafford. As a last resort Benaud switched to bowling his leg breaks from around the wicket and England lost their last nine wickets for 51 runs. So Australia won a Test match – by 54 runs – that they had seemed certain to lose. Back in the dressing room, Benaud just sat down with a beer with his mates and burst out laughing, a supremely happy man.

It also clicked for Mark Taylor in the semi-final of the 1996 World Cup in Mohali in northern India. Within an hour of the start Australia were 15-4 but they scrambled to 207-8; after 41 overs of their reply the West Indies were 165-2; yet Australia ended up winning by five runs. Inevitably Shane Warne, Glenn McGrath and Damien Fleming were to the fore as the West Indies collapsed in front of the increasingly alarmed eyes of their captain, Richie Richardson, at the non-striker's end.

I watched that match from afar and I have always been taken aback by one bowling change from Taylor. As the West Indies were cruising towards their target, he called upon Stuart Law, a part-time leg-spinner and the eighth bowler to be used in the innings. Law would end up bowling two nondescript overs for 13 runs and no wickets. Yet I've always marvelled at the bravado of Taylor in tossing the ball to Law at that time. This bowling change displayed a wonderful detachment. That semi-final was Australia's most important game of the year and they were losing it, but in dire straits Taylor was prepared to try something to turn the tide and, hell, it's only a bloody game.

Law was unable to change the course of the contest with the ball (though he had scored a vital 72 earlier in the day) but somehow Taylor's decision to bring him on has stuck in the memory. Australia's captain would not be hidebound by the occasion; rather than going through the obvious options, he would try anything, which included the unlikely ploy of 'giving Stuey a go' not for one over but two. It felt like a display of confidence rather than resignation, suggesting that the game was not yet over. Soon after Law's spell, a wicket was snatched and Taylor was able to pounce with his senior bowlers. The Australians held their nerve; the West Indies didn't. And no doubt he also laughed at the outcome with a beer with his mates afterwards 'in the sheds' of Mohali.

Maybe Taylor had almost given up in that semi-final. The cricket writer Martin Johnson, once of the *Leicester Mercury* before he was elevated to the *Independent* and the *Telegraph*, would often regale me with the story of how another great captain, Ray Illingworth, had given up the ghost on a slightly smaller stage, a John Player League game involving Leicestershire in the seventies. Not even Illy, the arch-tactician, could stem the opposition's run chase and so, with glum resignation, he tossed the ball to the off-spinner, Jack Birkenshaw. 'The game's up, Jack,' he said. 'You may as well have a bowl.' Birkenshaw proceeded to take 4-12 and somehow Leicestershire won. This meant that Johnson's report was headlined, 'Wily Old Fox Illy Conjures Amazing Win'. No doubt Illy was also smiling at the end, gently rewriting history but with warmer beer than Taylor.

I was also beaming when captaining Somerset after deciding to bowl Peter Roebuck at the death against the Combined Universities in 1989. A nasty humiliation at the hands of the students seemed inevitable in the quarter-final of the B&H

Cup, which would need some explanation. At Taunton the students required 30 more runs with seven wickets in hand, and just about every other option had been explored when I tossed the ball to Roebuck, an irregular bowler at that stage of his career. He obliged by bluffing a couple of batsmen out, including their centurion, Nasser Hussain. This was hardly Headingley '81 territory, I admit, but as a result of that desperate bowling change the old order somehow prevailed by three runs, an outcome that still rankles with the Universities' captain on that day, Mike Atherton. It would have been a major achievement for his side of students, albeit gifted ones, to reach the semi-finals of a domestic one-day tournament.

So the lure of captaincy is hard to resist despite all the brickbats around the corner. There were some obvious advantages. In the impecunious old days the captain was given extra expenses, with which he was expected to buy drinks for the players of both sides after the day's play; a source of even greater delight was that you could bullshit merrily after an unexpected win. More importantly, being captain meant you were definitely in the team for the next match except in the most extreme circumstances. (Mike Denness left himself out during England's 1974/75 tour of Australia, but a captain dropping himself is as rare as a politician's 'mea culpa'.)

The captaincy can enhance a cricketer. At Somerset, Brian Rose was transformed as a batsman once he was appointed captain of the club for the 1978 season. He gave up fretting about his place and grinding out his runs; instead he trusted his instincts and played his shots, which meant that he was a much more formidable batsman.

At Test level Illingworth suddenly became a significant run-scorer after being appointed captain in 1969 in an emergency when Colin Cowdrey had broken his Achilles tendon. Illingworth was, initially, regarded as the ideal stopgap, who would allow the easy return of Cowdrey once he had recovered fitness. He had just been appointed captain of Leicestershire but he was 37 years of age and at that stage in his international career he had played thirty Test matches in eleven years; he had not contributed many runs for England when in the team primarily for his bowling, and nor was his place ever secure. Illingworth was so successful that he kept the job until 1973, which meant Cowdrey was denied his desire to lead England in Australia – he ended up uncomfortably as Illingworth's vice-captain when the Ashes were won on the 1970/71 tour.

In fact, many Test captains experience an initial spike as a batsman – before exhaustion sets in. It can be liberating to have so much to think about beyond where your own next run is coming from. This applied to David Gower, Atherton and Alastair Cook at the start of their periods in charge. One oddity from my own experience is that I caught better when captain, which may have been a consequence of a desperation to restore order (a rare characteristic I share with Cook, who changed from being a bit of a liability in the field at the start of his Test career to becoming a very reliable first slip later on).

There is no identikit for the successful captain. There are no golden rules – except, perhaps, to be yourself. Compared to other sportsmen, cricketers spend so much more time with their colleagues on the road, in the dressing room and on the field of play. It is impossible to put on an act for all that time and still retain credibility among your peers. Do not make Gower captain if you're looking for an arch-disciplinarian; do not appoint Brian Close if you have identified the need for a careful conciliator.

At The Oval Robin Jackman was, in effect, Surrey's senior pro when Roger Knight took over as club captain in 1978. Knight was – and still is – an archetypal English gentleman. Educated at Dulwich College and Cambridge University, he would go on to be a public school headmaster, the chief executive of the MCC and then the president of the club. He was a 'Right then, chaps, let's get out there, fight jolly hard and give it everything we've got' sort of leader. At the outset Jackman felt obliged to point out that the Surrey team possessed some earthy cricketers who might not respond that well to stiff-upper-lip encouragements that had been honed on the playing fields of an English public school and at Fenner's. So he decided to take Knight to one side soon after his appointment and speak to him on the subject of team talks. 'I think you're going to have to eff and blind a bit or they won't have a clue what you're on about,' he said. It was well-intentioned advice but my impression is that Knight wisely ignored it and carried on being himself. They would have to respect him for who he was – and since he kept the job for six years at Surrey, we must assume this approach worked pretty well. For a few weeks Geoff Miller tried to be a stern, boisterous disciplinarian when succeeding Eddie Barlow at Derbyshire before realizing it was daft to try and imbue himself with his predecessor's characteristics.

Richie Benaud became cricket's Delphic oracle during the second half of his career and he famously observed that 'Captaincy is 90 per cent luck and 10 per cent skill. But don't try it without that 10 per cent.' We could quibble about the percentages but we know what he means. It is all about timing. It is no coincidence that the great captains generally had great players in their teams. Frank Worrell had the young Garry Sobers, Rohan Kanhai and Wes Hall; Clive Lloyd was blessed with Viv Richards, Gordon Greenidge and all those bowlers; Mike Brearley had the young Ian Botham, desperately hungry to prove his worth; Mark Taylor could always call upon Shane Warne and Glenn McGrath; so too could Steve Waugh (though he dropped Warne once). Michael Vaughan had Andrew Flintoff in his pomp; Eoin Morgan had Ben Stokes and Jos Buttler when England won the World Cup final in 2019; we may end up pointing out that in Test cricket Joe Root also had Stokes, who was so fiercely determined to atone for past misdemeanours. But take note: even the great players – at times especially the great players – need some sensitive handling.

A word here, a little detail there, is sometimes all that is needed from the captain. When Wes Hall ran in to bowl at Brisbane in the last over of the tied Test on 14 December 1960, Worrell quietly went over to his tireless fast bowler before the final delivery of the match and said, 'If you bowl a no-ball, don't go back to Barbados.' I assume there might have been a wry grin on his face at the time but I can't be sure; we know that Hall delivered the next ball with his foot a precautionary twelve inches behind the line before Joe Solomon went on to hit the stumps to run out Ian Meckiff with the scores level. Elsewhere, at Headingley in 1981, Brearley had a drink with Bob Willis on the fourth evening and told him to bowl as fast and straight as he could the next day and to 'forget about the no-balls' that had been plaguing him. So the good captains are flexible, adapting their advice to the situation, and they come in differing shapes, sizes and characters.

Brearley is one of the five most complete captains I have witnessed, mostly from beyond the boundary. Taylor, Vaughan, Eoin Morgan and Worrell are the others. My impression of Worrell is inevitably distant and sketchy. As a seven-year-old I followed England's 1963 series against the West Indies on the television and was transfixed; I even tried bowling left-handed because Sobers did. Only later would I recognize the enormity of Worrell's achievements: the first black captain of the West Indies who was able to forge the gifted cricketers of so many different countries in the Caribbean into such a formidable, entertaining side that helped to revitalize a flagging game. He just HAD to succeed, yet from afar he seemed so relaxed and composed when doing the job. Being the first officially appointed black captain of the West Indies surely made the burden borne by Len Hutton as the first professional to be appointed England captain seem like a feather weight, but you would never have guessed that from Worrell's calm demeanour. In between leading the side, he scored silky runs (a Test average just under 50) as well as taking a few wickets with his left-arm seamers.

The solitary downside for Brearley was the shortage of runs from his bat, and it is a testament to his captaincy skills that he carried on leading the side with authority anyway. Like Roger Knight, Brearley was a Cambridge graduate, an intellectual, who could easily have been a distant figure. Yet one of his attributes was his ability to get along with the earthier characters in his team; Ian Botham liked him a lot, respected him hugely and even did what he was told by him (most of the time). The same applied with Mike Hendrick, Geoff Miller, Derek Randall, Bob Willis and the rest who became stalwarts in a fine England side. As Brearley himself has acknowledged, he had far more problems pursuing a fruitful relationship with Phil Edmonds, a Middlesex colleague and Cambridge graduate. Even Geoffrey Boycott respected Brearley's opinion and his cricketing nous (if not his batting).

Geoff Miller has told me that when he was a young tourist, Brearley might knock on his hotel door and seek out his opinion about something. Miller recognized that Brearley would probably have already made up his mind but he wanted some input from a relatively junior member of the squad and he would listen to what Miller had to say. As a captain he was never in favour of the hierarchical system that had greeted him when he first played for Middlesex and Peter Parfitt, John Murray and Fred Titmus ruled the roost in the home dressing room at Lord's. So he could be a sympathetic captain, eager to consult and welcoming of alternative views, but he knew how to be tough as well. He might chide Wayne Daniel for not bowling enough bouncers for Middlesex; he might goad Botham for being the 'side-step queen' when he was bowling at less than full pace. At Headingley in 1981 he took Botham off after three overs and Ian was outraged:

'How can I bowl in three-over spells?' Brearley's response was: 'How can I bowl you if you bowl medium-paced half-volleys?' Botham, by the way, listened to criticism more readily than you might imagine – even though he gave very little indication that this was the case.

Brearley soon commanded respect and loyalty from his players and he relished the tactical challenges, the delicate balancing of attack and defence. It all seemed to come naturally to him; he knew the game inside out; he could provoke and sympathize with his players as required. He enjoyed the no-nonsense cut and thrust of the dressing room as well as the intellectual challenges the game threw up. Even a wrong decision might work out because his team had so much confidence in him.

It all seemed such a natural process for Mark Taylor as well. He never revelled in being the captain; he did not appear to covet the post, yet within months of his appointment he just seemed the obvious man to have in charge. Both Shane Warne and Glenn McGrath liked playing for him, which was vital to his success. Like Brearley, he stood at slip, quietly orchestrating everything while chewing his gum with Aussie vigour (unlike Brearley); this might include sticking Stuart Law on to bowl for no obvious reason. Then afterwards he would talk freely to the press in a matter-of-fact manner about the day's play as if giving an informal seminar. When his form failed, which was an issue at the start of the 1997 tour of England, he calmly acknowledged the problem rather than blustering and then he dealt with it. 'I still have the butterflies,' he said, 'but I now have them flying in formation.'

Michael Vaughan was not such a tranquil captain and was probably keener to do the job than Taylor ever was, after Nasser Hussain's sudden resignation in July 2003. For just over two years Vaughan was a brilliant captain, a man in the right place at the right time. Hussain and Duncan Fletcher, pitchforked together as strangers four years earlier, had done a lot of the hard yards, just as Allan Border and Bobby Simpson had for Taylor in Australia. Hussain had taken over in 1999 when the side was in disarray after a woeful World Cup campaign. At the end of his first campaign – a home defeat to New Zealand – the Test side was ranked eighth in the world and subjected to constant ridicule. Gradually Hussain brought order and discipline, revealing a flair for the job that surprised a few at the time, although I had been in the minority a couple of years earlier when advocating Hussain, rather than Alec Stewart, as Mike Atherton's successor.

With a solid, uncompromising platform laid, Vaughan was the ideal man to let the team blossom. In 1999 the England players needed to be reminded of some harsh realities and Hussain was good at that. By 2003, with Fletcher's strong arm firmly on the tiller, there was scope for a captain who was prepared to give the players more freedom to express themselves, to play a more expansive game, someone who would smile a bit more often. Vaughan was ready for the job and Hussain, an emotional man behind the screen, suddenly realized the lie of the land and went quickly in the middle of a series against a South African side led by Graeme Smith, who would soon gain a reputation for slaying most of England's best recent captains.

Vaughan had a sharp cricketing brain, a deep reservoir of self-confidence and some good players. But there was still some way to go to match an Australian side that had dominated world cricket for a decade. He had one other, even more important asset: the capacity to convince the team of 2005 that they really could beat Ricky Ponting's well-nigh invincibles and he realized that the only way to do it was to attack them. Playing the percentages would not work against the Australians with Warne and McGrath and co. They had to be assaulted, whether by Steve Harmison at Lord's, where England lost, or by Marcus Trescothick at Edgbaston, where they won by three runs. The consequence was the greatest Ashes series in history – and there are even Australians who acknowledge that. There was not a single dull day in five Tests as Vaughan and his team – with a bit of help from a stray ball here, a dropped catch there – held their nerve and prevailed.

Then it all fell apart as easily as a mild zephyr blowing away the whiskers of a dandelion. There were injuries in abundance, ill health and individual agendas. There would be no great legacy as there was with the West Indies side in the late 1970s and 1980s and Australia's in the 1990s and early 2000s. Suddenly Vaughan was scurrying around in the field, desperately waving a wand, looking for the magic solution, that moment of captaincy genius that we had all been reading about, to turn the game around. But it doesn't work like that, and the upshot was that Vaughan was becoming more reminiscent of Tommy Cooper than Merlin.

By now Monty Panesar had been added to the side, and when it was all starting to go wrong he seldom bowled to the same field for two balls in succession. Vaughan was forever manipulating, tinkering away with another change as he anxiously sought the magic elixir. But this only confirmed that he was beginning to lose control. His team disintegrated with alarming speed. Yet for two years from October 2003, they were terrific. During that time they won seven of their eight series (losing only in Sri Lanka), winning seventeen Test matches and losing just three.

I place Eoin Morgan in the highest category as a captain not just to show how modern I am. Yes, you can be a great captain exclusively in white-ball cricket. In fact, in some ways, captaining in a short-form match is more demanding than in a five- or four-day game. The shorter the contest the less time there is to think and consult. One extra over for a struggling bowler can be potentially devastating in one-day cricket, whereas in a Test match there is usually time to correct a tactical error. Morgan is decisive and often bold. ('Hellfire! He's just brought Rashid back at the death again.') His appearance remains icy cool whatever he feels inside and he backs his judgement; more importantly, so do the other ten out there. Unlike Hussain he was given the job *before* a woeful World Cup campaign, in Australasia in 2015, as the England hierarchy swerved by ditching Alastair Cook as their one-day captain just weeks before the tournament started.

Upon his return to England after that World Cup, Morgan was retained as the white-ball captain alongside a new coaching team of Trevor Bayliss and Paul Farbrace. Before long it was apparent that Morgan was the main man in the new one-day set-up. He devoted himself to every detail of the one-day game, a task assisted by the fact that he now rarely played any other form of cricket away from the international circuit beyond the burgeoning T20 leagues around the globe. He insisted that the team should play without fear – in fact, his coaches had said the same thing during the World Cup but had never backed this idea up with their selections or their plans. ('We'll play without fear... Gary Ballance is batting at three.') But Morgan meant what he said and this was evident from the uninhibited way he batted and by his sympathetic reaction to the odd inevitable failure of his teammates through over-ambition – the correct sort of shortcoming as far as he was concerned. There were no more cagey selections; Morgan wanted batsmen without hand-brakes – though some discretion from the likes of Joe Root was welcome. He wanted characterful bowlers who could bounce back from the indignity of watching another of their deliveries landing in the stands – as was ever more frequently the case in one-day cricket in the 2010s – and he wanted a varied attack, which usually meant the presence of Rashid's wrist-spinners and Moeen Ali's off breaks. He sought wicket-takers rather than containers.

Morgan never seemed ruffled even when the game was heading in the wrong direction. Increasingly it became clear that his players hung on his every word – even the coaches did – and they would follow him unreservedly. England's record improved with series victories galore in one-day cricket, but could they deliver in the more demanding environment of knockout cricket in ICC tournaments? Well, yes, eventually, sort of. The 2019 World Cup victory was the desired culmination of Morgan's work; he had created a team that never took a backward step with the bat, and that hung on combatively with the ball, one that never gave up and held their nerve after a few setbacks on the way to the final of the World Cup, their declared destination for three years. Even so, it remains something of a mystery how they won that game against New Zealand on 14 July 2019.

Morgan was happy to admit that he learned much from the Kiwis about building his team, in particular from their recent captain Brendon McCullum. They became close friends after playing together for the Kolkata Knight Riders in the Indian Premier League; McCullum was master of ceremonies at Morgan's wedding, which must have been an enjoyable occasion. The former New Zealand captain insisted that his cricket team should bring back the joy on the cricket field, a goal he achieved brilliantly and one that is much trickier than hosting a wedding celebration. McCullum demanded that his side should play a free-flowing game whether the ball was red or white and that they should respect their opponents and not bother with sledging, an attitude that caused some consternation in Australian ranks. Their wicketkeeper, Brad Haddin, for example, admitted feeling bemused by this new approach; it was anathema to a true blue Aussie. McCullum's ambitious plan worked and the game was so much better for that. That tradition has been superbly maintained by Kane Williamson, whose gracious acceptance that somehow New Zealand had lost that 2019 World Cup final was an act to match the heroics of any of the players on that day.

It takes all sorts, which makes the process of choosing a captain all the more intriguing. Some lead primarily by the sheer force of their personality. Brian Close and Tony Greig come into this category; both had charisma and a reservoir of self-belief that was way beyond the norm. Yet both were wise enough to listen. At Yorkshire, Close would take note of what Ray Illingworth and Jimmy Binks had to say (even though this may not have been entirely obvious to those looking on), and he might have listened to Tom Cartwright now and again when he was at Somerset in the wonderful autumn of his career. In the same way, Greig – a flamboyant figure and obviously the man calling the shots out there – was shrewd enough to seek the advice of Brearley, Keith Fletcher and Alan Knott, all cricketing sages who were probably standing alongside him in the slip cordon.

Away from England, Graeme Smith's dynamic personality was a factor in his astonishing longevity as captain. He led South Africa in 109 of the 117 Tests he played. At the start he was a noisy firebrand, but he mellowed out on the field once he recognized he had to give himself some space to think and, in any case, everyone soon knew who was the man in charge. He flew in and out of Taunton, briefly captaining a shy young Somerset side to a trophy in the T20 competition of 2005. He brought some of those youngsters out of their shells, sometimes by dragging them out of their rooms for a good night out.

Ricky Ponting may not have been a tactical genius – not too much of a hardship if McGrath and Warne are in your team – but he must have been an easy man to follow, such was his energy and passion for the game. Imran Khan may not have been quite so easy but in 1992 the Pakistan side that won the World Cup, despite being on the brink of an early and ignominious departure from the competition, were awed by his patrician presence, and finally 'the cornered tigers' broke free. Viv Richards had a similar impact in the West Indies dressing room after he succeeded Clive Lloyd. Somehow Imran and Richards were not men who invited argument.

Some of the larger-than-life personalities were not so popular outside of their own countries, partly because they refused to be cowed by the old order. Arjuna Ranatunga – unsurprisingly compared to Napoleon as he strutted around the square – always stood up for himself and his fellow Sri Lankan cricketers, which seemed to annoy the Australians especially. Unlike some of his predecessors, he would not passively give way to those who had run the game for decades. In the same way, Sourav Ganguly – 'Lord Snooty' to some – bowed to nobody and again it was the Australians who bridled the most; it infuriated Steve Waugh that Ganguly would always be late for the toss, which was a good enough reason for the Indian captain to ensure he always kept his opposite number waiting in the middle.

Ranatunga raised the World Cup in 1996 after a brilliant campaign culminated in victory over Australia in Lahore; the Sri Lankans outwitted their opponents as well as outplaying them. Ganguly led India to the final of 2003, when Australia won in Johannesburg. It may be that Sachin Tendulkar before him and Rahul Dravid afterwards were too polite and gracious for the role. Despite his patrician air, Ganguly had a gritty determination; he would not be pushed around by anybody. By the time M. S. Dhoni took over, no one was attempting to push around Indian captains; the power of India on the field (and, more obviously, off it) was now clear; they had good players to match the rest of the world and financial clout that was way beyond their rivals'. For the first time, India were in a position to dictate the path of the game, a role previously taken for granted by England and Australia. Hence Dhoni – the clearest thinking, coolest cat – did not need to challenge the status quo in the way that Sunil Gavaskar and Ganguly had done in previous decades. The status quo now suited India very well, thank you very much.

There have been great captains who did not necessarily have flamboyant, technicolour personalities but who were superb long-term strategists automatically trusted by the vast majority of their players. Andrew Strauss rarely reached for a rabbit from his cap and seldom stunned onlookers with the audacity of his latest plan. But he was clear, consistent and methodical in his approach; his players welcomed a man in charge with the steadiest hand on the tiller, calm in a crisis, who would put the team's interests first. Throughout his greatest achievement, retaining the Ashes in Australia on the 2010/11 tour, his team stuck earnestly to the plan to suffocate the Australian batsmen. Nothing fancy was required.

On that tour there was a minor issue with Kevin Pietersen, who was caught speeding around Melbourne in a Lamborghini sourced for him by Shane Warne. Without too much self-effacement, Pietersen explained how this little aberration had come about. 'This is Warnie's patch and when I'm in town he looks after me. Just as Sachin does in Mumbai and Ganguly in Kolkata.' The tour was going so well and this little incident would not be allowed to disrupt its progress, with Strauss pointing out that it would be boring if his team contained ten Strausses. It would also have been tricky with ten Pietersens. In fact, one Pietersen was more than enough to pose major problems at the end of Strauss's time in charge.

Clive Lloyd, who led the West Indies in seventy-four of his 110 Tests, was, like Strauss, more of a strategist than a wizard tactician. He departed on his own terms. He became a soft-spoken, avuncular presence by the end, whose toughness was well disguised. But he was undoubtedly the man in charge, uniting the brilliant cricketers from all around the Caribbean into a single-minded unit that would dominate world cricket for well over a decade. Sometimes he was criticized for his lack of tactical acumen, as if he were simply the foreman in the field, overseeing the rota for his awesome four-pronged pace attack. He just needed a reliable clock on the ground to make his bowling changes. It is true that the West Indies had a side that was often simple to lead in the field, but captaincy goes way beyond that. The longevity of the West Indies' success demonstrates Lloyd's qualities. He could be tough and principled, quietly putting any dissidents in the dressing room in their place when necessary; he was more inclined to douse the flames than stoke them.

'He is the calmest man I know,' said Viv Richards. 'It was a complicated thing to bring a West Indies dressing room together. Clive sent a message to the whole region: "Hey, West Indians can be happy together."' Joel Garner also summed up his impact on the dressing room neatly: 'He was a father, brother, friend. He was everything. He understood us.'

The warmth towards Lloyd extended to Manchester, his adopted home for many years. There they admired his batting and brilliant fielding and they soon came to enjoy his engaging sense of humour, which is reflected by one memory he shares of playing for Lancashire early in his career. Lloyd used to bowl quite frequently at a gentle medium pace – compared to the other West Indians. In the first ever World Cup final in 1975 he delivered 12 overs and was the team's most economical bowler. He also bowled for Lancashire as a youngster and he still recalls being summoned by captain Jackie Bond to bowl at the end where the umpire was Cec Pepper, who can be fairly described as a rough and ready, unreconstituted Aussie of the old school and something of a legend in the Lancashire League. Lloyd handed over his cap to Pepper, who bellowed down with an unmistakably Antipodean twang to the batsman at the other end: 'New bowler, change of action and change of colour.' Lloyd took no offence and still chuckles at the memory.

For shrewdness, look no further than Illingworth and Keith Fletcher. Both played in the era before the analysts set to work on their laptops, but Illy would insist that in the recesses of his brain he had files on every opponent. Fletcher was too modest to make such a claim but ask his

Essex teammates and they tell you that, while he could not remember anyone's name (and that often applied to members of his own side, let alone the opposition), he knew exactly how everyone on the circuit played. Illingworth was successful whether in charge of Leicestershire or England; Fletcher was an innovative, adventurous captain at Essex but was much less comfortable when elevated to the England captaincy and then, briefly, to the national coaching position. There the sense of adventure disappeared and he retreated into a bunker.

Some lead primarily by example. A display of guts and bloody-mindedness can be inspiring, and these were the key attributes of a range of captains. Allan Border never appeared to enjoy the job much, yet he did it for a decade and ninety-three Test matches, at the end of which Australia were a vastly improved side. Bob Willis – the rarest of breeds, since he was an out-and-out fast bowler entrusted with the job – drove himself to the absolute limits when captain. Mike Atherton and Alastair Cook were accustomed to leading England for years as opening batsmen, strapping on their pads sometimes after an exhausting couple of days in the field before facing the music once again. They would not dream of seeking refuge down the order. Just their longevity speaks of their toughness. Steve Waugh's tenacity would be reflected by the sweat seeping from his tattered, beloved baggy green. He inherited a very good side; even so, his record of forty-one wins from fifty-seven Tests as captain is astonishing. Virat Kohli's fierce and constant commitment is also awesome and he has already registered more victories as India's captain than anyone else, albeit in an era where draws have become very unfashionable.

Some captains have been surprisingly good. I have already mentioned Nasser Hussain, who was a success with England even though there were many who thought he would be too introspective and moody for the job. The same sort of sentiments applied to two of the best captains I played under below international level. Brian Rose at Somerset seemed the obvious choice afterwards but not necessarily at the time. He seldom said much in the dressing room when Brian Close was captain; he just concentrated on scoring his runs. It was hard to tell what he was thinking; occasionally we wondered whether he was thinking at all, which led – briefly – to the nickname 'dozy Rosey'. Once appointed, he did not suddenly become an extrovert firebrand but we soon realized he was tough, clear-minded and very determined, another strategist rather than an instinctive tactician, which meant he was quite an antidote to his predecessor. Many years later Tom Abell, thrust into the job with the minimum of experience, has demonstrated that he is one of those selfless, energetic and positive leaders whom players want to follow out onto the pitch.

Graeme Wood was my captain throughout the season I had as Western Australia's surprising choice of overseas player. In some ways he was similar to Rose: a self-contained character who did not waste words. His reputation prior to his appointment was of a tunnel-visioned cricketer, concerned only with his run-scoring – in short, a selfish batsman (though I should point out that selfish batsmen, provided they are any good, are a godsend to captains for 95 per cent of the time). But Wood's perspective changed with the captaincy; his prime goal was not scoring his runs but winning his games. Like Rose, he did not attempt Churchillian oratory yet his commitment to the cause and his intelligence were obvious. The system worked as WA won three consecutive Shield trophies from 1987 to 1989 under his captaincy.

There is, I suppose, one other category of captain that demands attention: those who do not appear to be very good at it – at least, if we only look at the figures. This list could be very long and it includes some very prominent cricketers, which is why we remember their struggles so well. The exalted names offer a reminder that the best players do not always make the best captains. Garry Sobers had a modest record as captain (he lost more games than he won); Brian Lara's return of ten wins and twenty-six losses in Test cricket is hardly a ringing endorsement of his leadership qualities (though by then the West Indies side had lost a lot of ammunition); Sachin Tendulkar captained India in twenty-five Tests, winning four and losing nine and was happy to pass the post on to somebody else and refocus his energy on scoring runs.

The Australians inevitably struggled during the Packer era. Graham Yallop was given a practically impossible task, which was to lead a virtual second eleven against Mike Brearley's tourists in 1978/79, and he did not do it very well. He lost the confidence of his best bowler, Rodney Hogg, who was soon proclaiming the virtues of Yallop's opposite number. 'He's got a degree in people,' said Hogg.

Any shrewd captain keeps his best bowler onside, although Jeremy Coney, a very shrewd captain, once led New Zealand to victory over the West Indies despite him and Richard Hadlee not speaking to each other at the time (emissaries were sent by Coney to ask whether Hadlee would like to bowl another over). Yallop was nicknamed 'Banzai' by the England camp because of the preposterously aggressive fields he often set. He was a fine batsman but his captaincy record of seven matches, one victory and six defeats does not lie. It was folly that the Australian selectors did not draw upon the leadership skills of John Inverarity during those Packer years.

Nor did the Australian selectors do their team any favours when they appointed Kim Hughes, whose record of four wins and thirteen defeats in twenty-eight Tests is not much better than Yallop's; they probably did not do Hughes any favours either. He was a brilliant, dashing batsman. He was also the golden boy of the cricketing establishment, untainted by signing up for Packer, and he was soon offered the captaincy after 'reunification'. It was well-nigh impossible for him to turn down such an offer; in fact, he was hugely excited by that possibility. What other reaction could there be for a young Aussie?

Hughes was charismatic, guileless, out of his depth and in the wrong place at the wrong time. His fellow West Aussies, Dennis Lillee and Rod Marsh, were still the dominant figures in the team and neither thought Hughes should be captain; both thought Marsh should be in charge in Greg Chappell's absence. Moreover, Hughes kept having to lead teams against the West Indies in their pomp. He resigned in tears in November 1984. In those days you might be pilloried for being a bloke crying in public in Australia. Real men did not do that then. Now it is a sure-fire way to gain the nation's sympathy. The relationship between the three West Australians made for a fascinating drama and was brilliantly explored by Christian Ryan in his book *Golden Boy*.

Around this time England had a few problems with the captaincy too. Ian Botham followed Brearley and it did not work. The evidence mounted up as Botham's form diminished and, like Hughes, he kept being confronted by the West Indies. In 1981 he experienced both torment and triumph. He resigned as captain, just before he was going to be sacked, after two Tests against Australia, which took him to a total of twelve matches as captain, none of which were won. Then, after the recall of Brearley, he played like a minor deity. There he was, supplying the most devastating evidence via his supernatural performances with bat and ball that he should never have been made captain in the first place. No wonder he has always had a love-hate relationship with that summer. At the time, Brearley felt Botham was the man to replace him in 1980; he wrote illuminatingly about this in a piece for the *Observer* thirty years after those epic performances at Headingley, Edgbaston and Old Trafford:

I am asked whether Botham could have had the phenomenal success of the rest of the summer [of 1981] – rightly they were called 'Botham's Ashes' – if he had not resigned as captain. I very much doubt if he could.

Was it a huge mistake for him to have captained at all? My view was that he had many of the qualities of a captain. He was shrewd tactically (characteristically erring towards attack). He was generous to players with far less skill than himself. He was courageous in speaking out frankly: for example he had helped Geoff Boycott when the latter was in a bad patch in Australia in 1978/9, and had ridden with good humour his constant banter about the stripes (corporal's ones) on his sleeves (Botham had been brought on to the touring selection panel). And he was a very different character to me. All of this was for the good. I was impressed. On the other hand he was young (24 when appointed), and entirely inexperienced in captaincy. He could occasionally become implacable in his disparagement of certain players. He could also get into arguments in public, even a brawl or two. I would have protected him a little by keeping me as captain for a few matches in the home series against the West Indies in 1980. I wrote to him in the West Indies the next winter with some advice: try captaining England against someone else. As it turned out it was, I admit, a mistake. He was too touchy about criticism. He found it hard to captain himself, to find that blend of restraint and liberation that I think he needed. Ian had fallen out with Graham Gooch over the amount of training he did (a great deal more than Ian, but none the worse for that). And the team had become demoralized; they had given up routines of practice. Worst of all, the pressure had got to him and England had lost the superb qualities of their best player.

Just about everyone thinks that now – except, perhaps, Ian. From a Somerset perspective, it is straightforward to confirm that Ian had a natural grasp of the rhythms of a game. On the field he could be innovative and encouraging, but at county level the job had many layers. In that era the captain ran the cricket for the club, and the solitary coach gathered the balls after practice. As an international cricketer, Ian had neither the time nor the inclination to do all that. In the end he had to be satisfied with being one of our greatest all-rounders but not one of our greatest captains.

Who should have been appointed after Brearley? Even with hindsight that is a difficult question. Bob Willis perhaps? He was already 31 and a fast bowler, who midway through that Headingley Test of 1981 thought he was playing his last match. I'm not sure that anyone was suggesting him at the time. Willis would become the most successful of a very unsuccessful bunch of England captains in the 1980s. At least he won more matches (seven) than he lost (five), which was not the case for those who followed him, David Gower and Mike Gatting. Like Brearley, Willis managed to avoid leading a side against the West Indies, which was a sure-fire way to have a poor record.

Gower replaced Willis and started well but his record disintegrated as he lost ten and drew two of his last twelve Tests in charge. I witnessed him at his best: in Pakistan on the 1983/84 tour after Willis was forced to return home early when he batted with grace and grit; in India the following winter when his side overcame many distractions – assassinations, the Bhopal catastrophe, a general election and the loss of the first Test in Bombay – to go on to win the Test series 2-1. On paper the side looked flaky (Botham was having a tour off) but he reintegrated the maverick Phil Edmonds, stayed calm amid the non-cricketing crises and refused to allow anyone to adopt too much of a siege mentality when it was all getting tricky. The following summer in England the Ashes were retrieved with Gower scoring 732 runs in a six-Test series, though nobody suggested the pursuit of the urn was being contested by the two best sides in the world. So all seemed hunky-dory until the West Indies, who accounted for ten of Gower's eighteen defeats as captain, were the opponents.

Gower was not capable of arresting a decline that became an undignified freefall against the West Indies. Then in 1989, against a more ruthless and disciplined Australian side, he led a motley team, half of whom had secretly agreed to head off to South Africa the following winter on another rebel tour. It was a shambles and not all Gower's fault but another shrug of the shoulders and the odd flip remark did not help much.

In the middle of Gower's two stabs at the job, Mike Gatting had the thrill of leading England to victory in Australia in 1986/87. The series was won 2-1 and these were the only two Test victories that Gatting enjoyed in twenty-three outings as a Test captain. If he was going to pick which two games to win during his time as captain, then the matches in Brisbane and Melbourne would be very good choices. He also led England to the World Cup final in Calcutta in 1987 when his reverse sweep to Allan Border's first delivery did not quite pan out as planned. Otherwise his was a remarkably cheerless reign, especially given Gatting's bubbly demeanour, punctuated by arguments in Pakistan and New Zealand and a lot of draws everywhere (he had the good fortune not to lead England against the West Indies).

Thereafter the England captaincy did not change hands with such regularity. It was as if fixed-term parliaments had been allotted to Graham Gooch, Atherton, Hussain, Vaughan, Strauss, Cook and Root, with a few fleeting intruders along the way. Those intruders struggled, and the most notable of those – Andrew Flintoff and Kevin Pietersen – soon gave further credence to the notion that the best players do not necessarily make the best captains. The pressures gnawed away at Flintoff on his Ashes tour in charge to the extent that he turned up for a morning fielding practice still worse the wear from an excess of alcohol on the previous night.

Subsequently Pietersen was candid about the demands of captaincy. In 2020, when commenting on whether Ben Stokes should captain England against the West Indies, he gave us an intriguing insight based on his own experience. 'You get looked at completely differently,' he said. 'Responsibilities change, communication changes, the way in which you carry yourself in the dressing room changes. It's a difficult place to be. I absolutely hated it. And I was rubbish. It's a completely different story.'

Both Pietersen and Flintoff had a natural understanding of

the game out on the field. But there is so much more to it than that. Which remains a source of fascination that other sports cannot match. I dread the day when the captain, armed with his earpiece, becomes the stooge out in the middle whose mundane job is to put into process the decisions of an omnipotent coach and his team of analysts hammering away at their laptops in the comfort of the dressing room.

3

Partnerships

'He obviously believed it was definitely going to happen.'

Jack Leach, Headingley 2019

'WE NEED TO bat in partnerships.' I've lost count of the number of times I've heard pundits make this sage observation. I've never thought this to be a very enlightening contribution. Rather, it seems a statement of the bleeding obvious. Of course we need partnerships because that means no wickets are falling. This analysis sits alongside the need to play 'smart cricket'. As opposed to what? Stupid cricket?

Yet there is a grain of truth there somewhere. How can the great batsman prosper at the crease and, perhaps, make history if he cannot find anyone to stay with him at the critical moment? Or in other fields, how would a comic genius like Eric Morecambe have fared if there had been no Ernie Wise? What would Brian Clough have achieved without Peter Taylor? Where would Wallace have been without Gromit? And I acknowledge I may be guilty of stating the obvious when pointing out how important Rod Hull was to Emu.

In cricket the most intriguing partnerships are among unequals, and sometimes the lesser cricketing mortals in those partnerships do not receive much attention so my plan here is to rectify that a little. For example, at Old Trafford in 1981 Ian Botham played what is universally regarded as one of his greatest innings against Australia. By his own admission, Ian had had a bit of a guffaw and a bit of a slog at Headingley two games before. Why not? The situation was somewhere between desperate and completely hopeless. Yet somehow it all worked out miraculously, with the ball flying everywhere from every part of his bat – and we all know what happened next. At Old Trafford almost four weeks later Botham produced an innings that had the purists purring as well, a classical display of aggressive batting that was so much more polished than his preposterous century at Headingley. But who were the men at the other end, running his singles – though there were not too many of them – and engaging in mid-wicket chats in between overs?

On both occasions Botham's partners were soft-spoken, self-deprecating men of Kent. At Leeds there was Graham Dilley, swinging his bat and guffawing almost as merrily as Ian. At that stage of his career Dilley was a dangerous hitter with a keen eye, although he regressed as a batsman at an alarming speed later in his career. At Manchester Ian had a rather more gifted, more calculating batsman at the other end: Dilley's Kent colleague, Chris Tavaré, an old friend of mine from the time we first met playing for England Schools. (As it happens, Chris was the man who gave a warm, heartfelt address in the cathedral at Worcester at the memorial service for Dilley in 2011.)

At Oxford University I had witnessed at first hand Chris playing some brilliant innings in the Parks, sprinkled with powerful drives all around the wicket. As I've tired of telling everyone over the years, he was not just a blocker; he had shots, especially in his youth, and throughout his career he delivered some of the most devastating one-day innings imaginable. However, at Old Trafford in 1981 he would stay true to his reputation. This was only his third Test match. He had played twice in 1980 against the West Indies but now, in the wake of England's two astonishing victories at Headingley and Edgbaston, he had been recalled to add a bit of stability to the batting line-up. In the first innings he contributed what *Wisden* describes as a 'stoic' 69 to enable England to reach 231; it took him four and three-quarter hours. England then bowled Australia out for 130 but they were labouring on the Saturday; just after lunch they had crawled to 104-5 from 69 overs when Botham, who had been dismissed for a duck by Dennis Lillee in the first innings, joined Tavaré in the middle.

This was Tavaré's first match under the captaincy of Mike Brearley and he has recalled walking out to bat with him after lunch with his nerves jangling: 'You would have expected our conversation to revolve around how we were going to cope with Lillee and co, but it didn't. Brearley knew that I'd studied zoology at Oxford and as we headed towards the middle he instigated a conversation about behavioural patterns. I'm sure this helped to relax me.' However, it did not do Brearley much good. He was soon caught down the leg side off Terry Alderman.

Cue Botham and his familiar bat-swinging entry into the arena. 'I have never experienced an atmosphere like that Old Trafford Test,' said Tavaré. 'There was a packed crowd and the Ashes were in the balance. When Botham entered, whirling his bat over his shoulders, the whole ground was transformed and the air of expectation among the spectators was enormous. They were not to be disappointed. Beefy started very slowly, which I always regarded as a good sign. His first 30 balls produced three singles and I remember saying to him between overs, "Are you trying to do me out of a job in this team?"'

Then Botham began to attack the left-arm spinner Ray Bright, taking two fours in an over. So Australia's captain, Kim Hughes, decided to take the second new ball, whereupon Botham exploded into action. Lillee put two men back on the leg-side boundary and bounced him. Botham hooked. Tavaré looked on with amazement. 'Each time I thought, "That's out" as the ball skimmed towards the fielder but it just kept going into the stands.' Lillee's first over back cost 22 runs, 19 of them from Botham's bat.

Tavaré described Botham's batting thereafter as 'savage'. 'I just sat back and watched, determined not to get out.' Botham's striking of a cricket ball was awesome on this Saturday afternoon, but his running between the wickets was not at its most reliable and there were a few close scrapes, which prompted Botham to say afterwards, 'I like batting with Tav. He seems to understand my calls even when I mean the opposite.'

Botham reached his century in 86 balls. At the time this was the fastest in England since 1902. When he was caught behind off Mike Whitney for 118, his partnership with Tavaré had been worth 149 runs in 123 minutes. The worth to the spectators lucky enough to be there was incalculable. Tavaré eked out a few more runs with Alan Knott before he was dismissed for 78 after seven hours at the crease. In all he had batted for twelve hours in the match for 148 runs. Afterwards Botham said, 'I got a lot of plaudits for my hundred but Tav never got due praise for his unselfish, determined batting in both innings.' Brearley recalled that Tavaré 'played one of his most stubborn, almost static, most invaluable innings'. But we all agree he was the support act here.

Australia fought hard in the final innings of the game, with Graham Yallop and Allan Border hitting hundreds, but England won by 103 runs. The Ashes were secure. So was Tavaré's place for another twenty-four consecutive Tests.

Our next support act scored even more slowly than Tavaré. Jack Russell at Johannesburg in December 1995 mustered 29 not out in four and a half hours. At the other end Mike Atherton was playing the innings of his life. This was the second Test match of England's first series in South Africa for thirty years. The first game at Centurion Park had been washed out but this one seemed to be heading South Africa's way. After surprisingly ponderous progress on the fourth morning, when only 20 runs were scored in the first hour, captain Hansie Cronje delayed his declaration until Brian McMillan had completed his century. By then, half an hour before lunch on the fourth day, the lead was 478. As Atherton and Alec Stewart strode out for the final innings of the match, there seemed to be plenty of time for South Africa to win.

Russell and Stewart were born in the same year (1963) and

both ended up as England wicketkeepers, but that is where the similarities end. Stewart was meticulously smart, the epitome of a modern professional sportsman, a stylish batsman who played silky strokes. Russell was never stylish in attire or at the crease. He could be quirkily superstitious, which meant throughout his international career he wore the same floppy hat that ended up like a scraggy patchwork quilt in varying shades of white, while ugly pragmatism was his trademark when batting. Yet both were terrific cricketers. Maybe they should have played together more often.

Russell appeared in fifty-four Tests; Stewart featured in 133 (eighty-two as the keeper, fifty-one as a specialist batsman). As a pure batsman Stewart averaged 46.70 for England; when keeping, this figure declined to 34.92. These are wonderful stats but they suggest England would have been better off if Stewart had always played as a pure batsman. After his retirement he told me that would have been his preference; he wanted to be an opening batsman, pure and simple, but circumstances (namely the need to conjure up an all-rounder from somewhere) intervened. So he took the gloves more often than not, a move that may have enhanced the number of caps he won but diminished his batting average.

Russell was no mean performer at this level with the bat, despite a technique as quirky as his floppy hat. He averaged 27.10 in Test cricket. Both were near their peak at the time of England's tour of South Africa. I talked to Jack a couple of weeks before that Johannesburg Test and it was obvious that he was now at ease within the England set-up, confident to be his own man. Which meant being unlike everybody else.

In May 1997 he published his autobiography, *Jack Russell Unleashed*, which upset some of those in charge of English cricket. In it there was confirmation of his nuttiness. The extracts serialized in the *Daily Mail* told us the following: Russell drinks thirty cups of tea and eats a packet of digestive biscuits per day; he insists upon his Weetabix being soaked for precisely twelve minutes; he has organized his own funeral not only with military precision but also a military presence (his coffin on a tank, Lee Marvin's 'Wandering Star' playing, plus a request for one of the royal family to attend); he wants his hands to be embalmed and displayed in a showcase in his art gallery; he is obsessive about his privacy; only his wife and his mother have his telephone number and visitors to his house have been blindfolded to prevent them finding their way back.

It may well be that in the intervening years Jack has modified some of these demands – though I hope not – but these were not the reasons why they were unhappy with his book at Lord's. The problem was that he had criticized Raymond Illingworth, who had become the self-styled 'One Man Committee' running the England team, by saying he was 'a lame duck', that he undermined the authority of captain Mike Atherton and that he was 'a failure' who opted to play golf with his batting coach, John Edrich, during the first training session of that South African tour.

My conversation with Jack at the start of the tour began with his two non-cricketing passions, military history and painting. He had just returned from visiting Sanna's Post, a battlefield of the Second Boer War, which is near Bloemfontein, no doubt with his easel for company. He explained that his painting had kept him sane especially on those long tours when he was the second wicketkeeper. But now he was the Test wicketkeeper with Stewart opening the batting even if he sensed that Illingworth was not his greatest fan. He explained how the most traumatic period of his career had been in 1994 when Illingworth plumped for the Yorkshireman, Steve Rhodes, as his Test keeper. 'Before that I had been dropped but always for a batsman [like Stewart and Richard Blakey, a calamitous pick for the tour to India in 1992/93] in an effort to improve the balance of the side. But Rhodes had an identical role to me. It was a straight choice; they preferred him and it hurt.'

Russell returned to the England side in 1995 'with a mission, no longer frightened to get out and determined to play my own way'. At Old Trafford he guided England to victory against the West Indies in the fourth innings; at Trent Bridge, when it was uncertain whether Atherton was going to be fit to play, he was asked whether he would lead the side. His response: 'Yes. I'll have some of that,' and on the eve of the match he made his plans right down to what he would say to the BBC's Tony Lewis after the toss. However, Atherton was fit to play. In the meantime Russell would continue to plough his own furrow, oblivious to what his coaches or his opponents might think of his quirks, which now included his exaggerated 'curtain rail' leave to balls outside his off stump. As if anticipating his role alongside his captain in those memorable two days in Johannesburg, he said, 'I am one of the leaders now. Athers doesn't have to tell me that.'

In that second Test, Russell had already taken a record eleven catches when he joined Atherton at the loss of England's fifth wicket at 11.45 a.m. on the final day. By then Atherton had reached his century – but could anybody stay with him? At first it did not look as if Russell would manage that. Before lunch he was all at sea, spooning a delivery from Shaun Pollock tantalizingly over short leg; he was also dropped by Meyrick Pringle in his follow-through. But Russell survived until the interval, when his skipper – who had now been batting for almost seven hours – offered some encouragement: 'They'll start twitching if they don't get a wicket in the next session.'

They didn't get a wicket in the next session. Russell was more secure after the break when the left-arm spinner, Clive Eksteen, occupied one end while the pacemen rotated at the other. After the mid-session drinks interval, twelfth man Richard Illingworth reported back to the dressing room that 'Jack's looking knackered but Athers is as fresh as a daisy.' This pair were still together at tea when Atherton recalled, 'the mood in the dressing room was still tense, but more upbeat. We had come so far that the thought of losing the match now made me sick in the stomach. This was a different sort of pressure, the worst kind. Now it would be a massive cock-up if we failed to save the game.' Next man in, Dominic Cork, was still in the chair that he had been occupying for almost three hours, suffering similar agonies.

Back in the middle, Atherton remained in sublime control while Russell, even though he was barely scoring any runs, was warming to his task. Atherton remembers, 'Jack kept reminding me of Barbados 1990 – even though I wasn't there

– when we lost five wickets in the final session [after another brave, though ultimately unsuccessful, rearguard action with Russell to the fore]. He kept badgering me to stay in during that final session.' At the end Atherton recalls Bob Woolmer, South Africa's coach, congratulating him graciously, being engulfed by his players and receiving a handshake from Illy, who described his knock as 'one of the greatest of all time'. Illingworth was rarely so effusive about a modern player.

There was one more surprise in store for Russell. To Jack's astonishment, he discovered that John Barclay, the tour manager, had surreptitiously flown his wife out to Johannesburg in time to greet him back at the hotel, which completed what he described as the 'two greatest days of my life'.

Years later I spoke to Atherton about his innings. He was not being arrogant when he suggested that such a knock might never be played again. 'There are several players around now who could play that type of innings,' he said. 'Andrew Strauss could. I'm sure Sachin Tendulkar and Rahul Dravid could. So might Mike Hussey. But they probably would not do so. Today they would be going for the win. In 1995 we never thought about winning that Test. It never occurred to us that it was feasible. That's changed. Expectations have risen. Sides have proven that you can chase 400-plus successfully.'

Not very often, though. At Headingley in 2019 England, who had been bowled out for 67 by Australia in their first innings, needed 359 to win the match. After their first innings debacle, I was asked by one young scribe as I was leaving the ground whether I had 'finished' the England team in my piece. 'Let's wait and see who wins the match first,' I replied. It was probably a stupid, curmudgeonly thing to say, although, like Atherton, I'm now of the opinion that the modern player is rarely intimidated by any target. And there was plenty of time left in this game.

So far our support players have somehow failed to match the preferred identikit of the modern professional sportsman. Tavaré was too self-deprecating, while Russell was too scruffy, and the pattern is neatly sustained by our third unlikely accomplice, who witnessed an astonishing innings by Ben Stokes from a distance of 22 yards. It was Jack Leach, the bespectacled, slightly cumbersome left-arm spinner from Somerset, who provided a memorable support act, delivering arguably the best one not out in the history of the game.

You will recall the scenario. Already Stokes had played a stunning innings (although his run-out of Jos Buttler had been a bit of a hindrance to the run chase) but at the fall of the ninth wicket (Stuart Broad lbw to James Pattinson for a duck), 73 more runs were needed as Leach made his way to the middle. In the press box at Headingley, a converted lecture theatre, the contingent of Aussie pressmen had just woken up. They had endured an uncomfortable afternoon but now they sensed that order had been restored; an Australian victory was on the horizon and their impersonations of church mice had come to an end. When Stokes hit a six, one of them, who had rediscovered his voice, shouted out with glee, 'You only need a dozen more of those.'

Once again, we all know what happened next, with Stokes moving into overdrive and producing a range of astonishing shots that kept clearing a very heavily populated boundary.

Here was melodrama that no scriptwriter would dare to pen. Roy of the Rovers never pulled off such a spectacular victory as this. But what must it have been like for the bloke at the other end? In the following days and months Jack Leach did his best to let us know, while the nine-year-old Rebecca Close, in an award-winning piece in the *Guardian*, was inspired to write from the perspective of Leach's glasses: 'There is only one man left and that happens to be my owner... the atmosphere was intense as I jiggled up and down on Leach's nose... every two seconds I would be temporarily blinded by a cloth wiping across my face.'

Leach offered confirmation that Rebecca was on the right track: 'The crowd there was amazing. I've never experienced an atmosphere like that.' Stokes was amazing, too. 'Unbelievable,' said Leach. 'Walking out with 73 to win, I don't know if you can believe you can do it.' He could not quite remember the exact details of his conversation with Stokes upon arrival in the middle:

I think he spoke about the plan, how we would go about it. Straightaway he was thinking how we would knock off the runs. He obviously believed that it was definitely going to happen. It seemed that simple. I can't remember who was bowling; Pattinson, I think. Ben said: 'Watch hard and try to get to the end of the over.' After that he told me how I was going to face one or two balls an over and to back up, to look for two.

I managed to get to the end of that over. It is all a bit of a blur, to be honest. And yet I've never been so focused as at Headingley. I never looked any further than the ball I was facing. I didn't want to get in Stokesy's bubble when he was hitting those sixes. I didn't want to say too much. I just wanted him to focus on every ball and if it was there, hit it for six. I just had to stay calm and do the job at hand. I felt good; I was really focused on what I needed to do.

Staying calm for Leach meant giving some attention to those glasses. 'I just had to make sure they were clean every time I was facing because I would really regret it if they had been smudged. [After the game the Test sponsors, Specsavers, promised to supply him with free glasses for life at the suggestion of Stokes.] Suddenly it's eight to win and you're like "Oh my God." Ben said in the changing room afterwards that this was when he got nervous.'

Australia were now in panic mode as well. They wasted an lbw review against Leach when the ball clearly pitched outside his leg stump; Leach should have been run out but Nathan Lyon fumbled the ball at the bowler's end; Stokes looked to be plumb lbw but he was given not out and there were no reviews left for the fielding side. Then Leach stole his single on the leg side off Pat Cummins to level the scores before Stokes pummelled the winning cover drive. It was one of those rare occasions as a journalist where one did not begrudge the necessity of having to rewrite completely. David Gower – not known for hyperbole – said Stokes's effort was 'the most incredible innings by anyone, ever'.

It was hard to argue with Gower. That Stokes innings surely

outstripped the ones by Botham in 1981, but that was a silly argument for another day. The nation was mesmerized. Stokes was happily reinstated as a national hero. And I was able to inform Leach that he was suddenly a cult hero after facing 17 deliveries and scoring one vital run.

'That's nice,' he said. 'I don't really know what that is. It's probably because I look like a village cricketer out there with my glasses, the bald head and maybe people think: "That could be me." All the others look pretty professional.' Perhaps it was the glasses and the distinctive gait. Somehow he brought to mind the 'bank clerk who went to war' for England in 1975, David Steele. Leach has proven himself to be a Test-class spinner, yet somehow with the bat in his hand he was accessible to all those eager amateurs who take to the field on a Saturday afternoon. None of us could emulate what Stokes did that day, but in our daydreams doing what Leach did at Headingley was just about possible.

Leach himself seemed to understand that. 'I only got one not out, but just to be part of that day and to see how it affected so many was a special thing. People kept telling me where they were when it all happened. They didn't even like cricket but they were following it. I loved being part of that series,' he says. 'I learned an awful lot in county cricket about the game. At international level you learn about your own game and yourself. It tests your character more than anything.'

Leach is undoubtedly a cricketer of character. He had demonstrated that many times before that match in Leeds. Along the way he has had to overcome untimely injuries and illness, having been diagnosed with Crohn's disease at the age of 14, as well as surprising question marks about the validity of his action. He keeps going regardless and, whatever happens next, he will always have that surreal Headingley afternoon.

4

The Spell

'It was perfect when it left my hand.'

A spinner's lament

IT MUST BE about time for me. No wickets have fallen for a while, the pacemen are starting to look as if they need a break, and in all probability it is not long before lunch. Time for the spinner. I start loosening up not too ostentatiously – I don't want the captain to think I'm being too presumptuous, that I'm telling him he has already delayed my introduction for far too long – but I want to be ready.

I'm eager to join the action, to be part of the game, and the sooner the better. It's the waiting in cricket that can be such a torment. You never know when you're going to bat and as a spinner you often never know when you're going to bowl. At least an opening batsman and an opening bowler are usually spared that nagging uncertainty.

Think of Michael Holding ahead of that over in the Test match at Barbados against Geoffrey Boycott in 1981. He knew when he was going to bowl. So off he went with the little, teak-hard Aussie physio, Dennis Waight, to get himself ready. Waight put him through his paces, ensuring that every relevant muscle was fine-tuned. When the England innings started, Holding was perspiring nicely and his body was loose; it was as if he had already bowled three overs. As a consequence he knew that his opening spell would have to be short but it might be deadly. And it was. Holding was at full throttle from the very first ball and he was on target.

Boycott was by now 40 years of age yet his wicket still somehow counted more than the others in the England side. 'I never laid bat on ball in five deliveries and then he knocked my off stump over with his sixth,' recalled Boycott, who added that the most disconcerting thing about batting against Holding was 'you always felt he could bowl a little bit faster if he wanted to.' In Barbados in front of a packed house, Holding was perfectly prepared to deliver something devastating.

More often than not the spinner is denied the luxury of knowing exactly when his spell is going to start. The old-timers were more canny than cavalier in approach to their opening overs. The Worcestershire, Warwickshire and England left-armer, Norman Gifford, who toured with England as the assistant manager in the 1980s, always stressed how important it was to lay a good base, not to be too profligate or too ambitious at the start of a spell. There must be no easy runs for the batsman, no experiments until rhythm and accuracy had (hopefully) been established. The idea was to stay on and to put the pressure on the batsman. This all made excellent sense to me and generally it was what I tried to do in my first few overs. Before my first Test match, Ray Illingworth kindly offered similar advice: 'Don't go overboard with men around the bat early on – just because you're now a Test bowler.'

Spinners of Illy's era were expected to be miserly and the best ones were. English off-spinners would bowl a cagey line, offering the batsmen no width to hit the ball through the off side. Fred Titmus, Illy himself and later John Emburey preyed on the batsmen's patience; there would be no free runs. Left-armers like Gifford and the great Derek Underwood would be equally mean. The same applied with the beguiling Indian finger-spinners, Bishan Bedi and Erapalli Prasanna, even when they were conjuring up their beautiful variations. Accuracy was automatically anticipated – the *sine qua non*, as Illy, Giff and Embers didn't used to say.

It would be tedious if everyone adopted such a cautious approach, though. Step up, Shane Warne, at 3.06 p.m. on 4 June 1993 in Manchester, for his twelfth Test match for Australia and his first against England. The previous eleven had taken place on the other side of the world, so the alarm bells had not been ringing that loudly in the northern hemisphere. Before that Ashes tour Martin Crowe had announced that Warne was already the best leg-spinner in the world, but this was England, where wrist-spinners seldom prosper. Early in the tour young Warne had played at Worcester, where he opted to keep some of his tricks up his sleeve and, after Graeme Hick had hit a second-innings century, he finished with modest figures of 1-122. But after his appearance on that second afternoon of the first Test of the series at Old Trafford, the cricketing world would never be quite the same again. Warne was hardly the epitome of caginess as he prepared to deliver his first ball in Test cricket on English soil. Mike Gatting was the batsman, renowned as an excellent player of spin bowling. We all know what happened next, although it took some time for Gatting himself to come to terms with a nightmarish sequence of events. Warne says in one of his autobiographies, 'In the second or so the ball took to leave my hand, swerve to pitch outside leg stump, fizz past the batsman's lunge and clip off stump, my life did change.'

There was no canny compromise from Warne at the start of his spell. We know how that ball zipped out of his hand and how it would be dubbed – with some justification – the ball of the century. And we remember how Gatting, once he had ascertained what had happened, which took a while, departed like a man betrayed. The easy conclusion is that this one delivery sums up the irrepressible cavalier that is Warne. In fact, it is not quite that simple. Warne was not just a cavalier; he was streetwise as well, and cavaliers are not supposed to stoop to such pragmatism. Yes, he oozed confidence as he fizzed that first delivery; he was on the attack from the start. Even at a young age he would stare down the batsman, get under his skin, suggesting that the fall of another wicket was imminent and inevitable. He would hint that his bag of tricks was limitless, with talk of zooters and mysterious wrong'uns (he had a googly but it was not a great one) to augment his fast, dipping leg break and the flipper that wasn't a long hop after all. He had enough tools, all right, but he also had attitude and he was brave, forever up for the challenge whoever was batting.

Yet he had other important virtues not always associated with the cavalier. He was accurate, incredibly accurate for a wrist-spinner, in a manner that would have greatly impressed Ray Illingworth a few decades before. There was no easy escape for the batsman to the other end – and even if he got there, Glenn McGrath was probably bowling. Moreover, Warne would recognize when batsmen were reading him well, picking up that googly and plonking it to the mid-wicket boundary. If the runs were coming too freely he would say, 'Round the wicket, ump,' and from there he would aim into the rough outside of the right-hander's leg stump and challenge the batsman to score any runs from there. The only option was a risky sweep with the odds in Warne's favour.

It was almost a compliment to the batsman when Warne used this ploy, and against England he did it most often to their best players – Graham Gooch initially and then, later in Warne's career, Kevin Pietersen. In essence it was a negative move that might result in the batsman kicking the ball away time and time again. Yet, when Warne was doing this, it was rarely interpreted as such; it was another cunning plan. When Ashley Giles bowled outside leg stump to Sachin Tendulkar in Bangalore in 2001, the tactic was roundly condemned. (It was very tedious, though it eventually led to Tendulkar being stumped for the first time in his Test career, as neither Giles nor captain Nasser Hussain were minded to be swayed by any complaints from the purists.) This is not to condemn Warne but to point out that he was not a one-dimensional cavalier; he was extraordinarily astute as well – and the best spin bowler I've ever seen.

That first delivery at Old Trafford was astonishing. Oddly I can find vaguely common ground with Warne here. Surprisingly often, the first ball I bowled in a spell turned more than any of the subsequent ones. In my case – as opposed to Warne's – this must have been because I was not particularly trying to spin the ball and it may have built up false hopes; I was just aiming for the right spot; my fingers were not straining to impart spin, which meant they may have been more relaxed. It is, you'll agree, a distant parallel. A closer one might be provided by Graeme Swann.

Swann took wickets in the first over of a spell so frequently that it cannot have been a coincidence. He was/is never short of confidence and he was prepared to rip the ball from the outset; he may have reasoned that, while he was at his most vulnerable at the start of his spell, so too was the batsman. And he was ever-optimistic; he always thought a wicket was around the corner. 'I aim high from the word go,' he says. However, his aim when he bowled his first ball in Test cricket, in Chennai in December 2008, was not great. 'The first one felt like I had a ping-pong ball in my hand,' he recalled later that evening. 'It was a terrible delivery. My mum could have hit it for four [in fact, the Indian opening batsman, Gautam Gambhir, did]. Then it all went a bit crazy.' Gambhir was lbw to Swann's third delivery, and with the sixth Swann took the even more prized wicket of Rahul Dravid. So he set off for tea with figures of 1-0-7-2. He was on his way to becoming England's second-highest wicket-taker among spin bowlers – after Derek Underwood.

There was no great mystery about Swann's bowling; he did not pretend to possess a zooter or a doosra. But he had many virtues. He spun the ball vigorously, which makes it dip as well as turn (that dip is just as important, by the way, since it makes judging the length of the delivery much more difficult), and he bowled a brave line that challenged both edges of the bat. Illingworth and Emburey would have been wary of offering the right-handed batsman so much width so often. He was also optimistic. And canny.

He would probably acknowledge that the advent of the DRS helped him significantly; indeed, it rejuvenated the art of finger-spin at a time when it seemed to be becoming increasingly redundant. Lbw Swann or lbw Panesar became common dismissals, with Swann tormenting left-handers and Panesar right-handers. For years finger-spinners had been frustrated by the front pad of cagey batsmen. They pushed forward in defence with bat and pad locked together and the umpires refrained from giving them out because 'they're too far forward, son.' Sometimes those batsmen were only pretending to play a shot, but how could the umpire be sure of that? There was a bit more hope when the umpires were bowlers – especially ex-spinners like Sam Cook, who, having been frustrated for so long in their own career, now demanded a more moral approach to batting. If the batsman was swinging across the line, albeit on the front foot, there was a chance of an lbw on the basis that such a heathen shot should be punished and deterred by a raised finger. However, unless Sam or one or two like-minded souls were umpiring, those lbws could be hard to come by.

But in Swann's era the tracking system demonstrated that so many of those deliveries were hitting the stumps as well as fulfilling all the other necessary criteria. Batsmen had to learn to use their bats again. I once asked Ray Illingworth how many more wickets he would have taken with the DRS in place. He thought long and hard – as he would – and replied, 'About 500'. I was inclined to agree with him (although my additional tally would have been nowhere near that many). Nonetheless, I wasted a lot of energy in my career appealing for those lbws.

Back to my spell. Being from the pre-Warne/Swann era and, more importantly, unable to give the ball such a vigorous tweak even in my pomp, my main concern was to land the damn thing in the right place in that crucial first over. If it was spinning nicely then that was a bonus. It is hard to underestimate the importance of that first over. If it was poor and properly punished I was condemned to playing catch-up from the start, trying desperately to regain control. The first goal was to bowl well enough to stay on. To mirror the genteel though not so gentle reprimand delivered to Harold Abrahams in *Chariots of Fire* by his girlfriend, Sybil ('If you don't run you can't win'), if you don't bowl you can't take any wickets.

I'm tempted to advocate a remarkably time-consuming form of practice for a spinner: to bowl an over and then to disappear for a quarter of an hour or more for some more fielding practice before returning to bowl another one. Logically this should enhance the ability to produce a satisfactory first over from scratch even though it takes up a lot of time. A first-over maiden is precious and less frequent than in the dull old days. Batsmen are not so well behaved now. They are less likely to play everything on merit. Especially against novices, their inclination is to launch an early attack, to hit a good ball for four or six via an old-fashioned lofted drive or a trendier reverse sweep and thereby puncture the confidence of the young bowler right from the start of his spell. In the 1970s and 1980s that was the exception rather than the rule.

Once in the groove, I want a wicket. Of course I want a wicket. After half a dozen overs I may be getting desperate for a wicket, though it's best not to show it. Now the temptation is to go searching. Do I need to toss the ball higher, somehow try to spin it more, to bowl slower or faster or from a different angle? The answer of the non-cavalier is 'probably not'. Retaining that pressure on the batsman is more important. More wickets come from batsman error than an unplayable delivery; that is certainly the case lower down the scale but it still applies (albeit less frequently) at the highest level.

I was once bowling to Alvin Kallicharran, the West Indian left-hander, who was playing for Warwickshire, and I was bowling rather well. Kallicharran was a very high-quality player but he was not scoring freely; I was not beating his bat but, by the same token, he was not beating my field and I was pleased by that. But then the delusions of grandeur creep in. I know, I'll toss one higher in the air, almost as a demonstration of my new-found prowess and confidence. I was quite pleased with the delivery as it left my hand but Kallicharran spotted the change of speed and trajectory in an instant, skipped down the pitch and hit it for four. The great players do not need much time to do that. Any pressure had now dissipated and I could only chastise myself for that. 'Why are you trying to be so clever? Leave that to the armchair spinners – or Bishan Bedi.'

Those armchair spinners can be destructive. Monty Panesar had one of the best natural actions imaginable, strong in the shoulders and the fingers. He was the ideal bowling machine. The ball could fizz out of his hand and dip and spin at speed – at over 55 mph. (Out of curiosity I would have loved the benefit of a radar gun when I was playing – though the spin-cam gadget, which measures how rapidly the ball was rotating, would perhaps have been less welcome.) Soon the sedentary sages were urging Panesar to bowl more slowly and with more variety. Terrible advice. Monty had a natural pace, which was quick and potentially lethal on turning pitches. It was so counterproductive to encourage him to bowl more slowly, something he wasn't very good at. Besides, it is easy to forget 'natural variation', the sort that just happens because bowlers are not robots; only the very gifted can change to order. Underwood once described himself as 'a low-mentality bowler', reluctant to experiment, and by and large this was a virtue for him rather than a shortcoming. In this era spinners – especially finger-spinners – are getting quicker. Nathan Lyon now bowls much faster than when he started playing for Australia; this also applies to Jack Leach and Dom Bess. In that sense, Panesar was ahead of his time. As we have already noted, they all aim for the front pad now and a successful lbw appeal as well as the edge of the bat.

Hang on, it's turning. This is a realization that can prompt two reactions from the bowler. The first, which is the best and appropriate one, goes as follows: rub hands together and issue a reminder to self that this is my day, that I've been waiting for a surface like this to bowl on for weeks/months. The odds are in my favour. Yes, it's going to be my day. Nothing clever is required (save that for the flat tracks) because the ball is turning. Pin them down and, with patience, the wickets will follow. The second reaction? Blimey that was a surprise; that spun sharply. Oh no, they are all expecting me to bowl 'em out now. My less sympathetic colleagues are already saying, 'You're bound to get a five-for here.' That's not really fair. When the pitch is green and seaming there are usually three pacemen on call to do the needful but I'm the solitary spinner in the side. Everything depends on me and now I've just over-heard one of our batsmen saying, 'How come it was spinning so much more quickly when they were bowling?' I'll get some flak if I don't bowl them out here.

What would I give for an early wicket? It can come from a long hop, a full toss or an unplayable delivery that brushes the shoulder of the bat. It just settles the nerves, whoever you are. This applies to Jimmy Anderson and Derek Underwood as well as me. With an early wicket under the belt, I can stop straining; patience is not so hard to find. Torment those batsmen. Make sure they have nothing easy to hit and then the likelihood is that they will counter-attack on a difficult surface; disrupting my rhythm, breaking my control is their best chance of survival. I'll accept the odd swing over the boundary from a blameless delivery that was 'perfect when it left my hand'. The odds are still in my favour even if the batsman decides to counter-attack.

I can recall just two instances when everything went abso-lutely to plan when the ball was turning – and don't think you are going to escape without my mentioning them. The first took place in Perth, Western Australia, which is supposedly a haven for pacemen. It was not a first-class match but the standard was reasonably high. On 21 November 1981 I was playing first-grade cricket for Bayswater Morley against Claremont Cottesloe. Bruce Reid, soon to be Australia's opening bowler, had failed to make any inroads for our side, but when I was introduced it transpired that the ball was turning more than was usually the case in this part of the world. Even so I did not take a wicket until my ninth over, which provides statistical evidence of the need to be patient. At this point our opponents were 50-1.

I know all this because, before I left Perth that winter, I was presented with the scorecard at the end of the season and I'm looking at it now. It reveals that on this strange day I finished with figures of 34.1-21-28-9 for Bayswater Morley in the first-grade competition. Claremont Cottesloe were bowled out for 118 after facing 87.1 overs. It's hard to credit; I remember the outfield was slow, the boundaries long, the ball turned, though not that spitefully, and towards the end of their innings paranoia had set in among our opponents; they blocked and they slogged but there was nothing in between. They felt trapped and they could not see a way out. On a good day, spinners can have that impact; in fact, I've seen it happen at Taunton a few times recently (long after my retirement) when Jack Leach and Dom Bess have held sway.

The other occasion when it was all so simple and inevitable was in a first-class match that took place in Bath in 1985, a dreadful season for Somerset. There had been heavy rain, which forced us to use the same surface for our second

Championship match of the Bath festival. To make matters worse, I think earlier in the summer the local groundsman had mistakenly sprinkled weedkiller rather than fertilizer on the square. Needless to say, the ball was spinning a lot by the final day of the match against Lancashire, and I have the figures from their second innings to prove it: 22-15-17-8. It may have helped that they had three left-handers, albeit pretty good ones in their side: Graeme Fowler, Neil Fairbrother and John Abrahams. But the odds were in my favour again. There was no need for any clever variations: a persistent line and length was sufficient and, once the dominoes started to fall, they all found a way to get out. It was never as straightforward again. That 8-17 was probably no better than a long-forgotten 3-60 on a flat track. But at least on that occasion I must have rubbed my hands together in the approved manner because it was my day.

Moeen Ali had been denied this kind of experience on the county circuit when he was plucked out by England. He had never been Worcestershire's primary spinner, although he had established himself as one of their best batsmen when he made his Test debut against Sri Lanka at Lord's in 2014. No wonder he would suffer from a few identity issues as a Test player.

Moeen is one of my favourite cricketers. Off the field he has been one of England's most reliable men. They all say he is a rock-solid character, forever giving to the team, selfless, cheerful and mischievous, a constant benign influence in the dressing room. Out in the middle, reliability has seldom been the first word that springs to mind when Moeen is at the centre of the action. He can bat beautifully, timing a cover drive like

Gower in his pomp, and in a perfect world he would have ended up batting somewhere in the top six for England and bowling when the occasion demanded. Yet that never happened. He was in the Test team – to his mild surprise – primarily for his bowling despite such limited experience, although there was obvious potential for Moeen the off-spinner. His stock delivery has all the right ingredients: it spins vigorously at a good pace and it often dips at the end of its flight path. But we are never quite sure how the ball will come out of Moeen's fingers. He is a self-effacing bowler partly because he was never accustomed to being Worcestershire's main spinner and so he has not always looked comfortable in his role for England when the ball is turning and he is expected to bowl out the opposition. We should not be so surprised by that. Unlike Swann, who was exiled from the England set-up for almost a decade (he would never have returned if Duncan Fletcher had stayed on longer), Moeen had to learn how to be a Test bowler on the job.

Nor does he hint at any guile. The simple fact is that most spinners suggest a lot more guile than they actually possess. A smile, an exasperated glance or a knowing look might give the impression that the last boundary conceded was in fact all part of an elaborate, cunning plan. Such bluffing is an important element in the spinner's armoury. Given that he can't propel bouncers – although Phil Edmonds managed to deliver a few in his time – these mind games represent much-needed ammunition for the slow bowler. But Moeen does not indulge in such fancies because he never nurtured them in the anonymous nursery of county cricket. It looks as if he meanders up to the crease, gives it a rip and hopes for the best.

And still, despite all that, only three English spinners have taken more than Moeen's 189 Test wickets (as I write): Derek Underwood, Graeme Swann and Jim Laker. Among those spinners who have taken 100 wickets for England only Swann can match Moeen's strike rate. Admittedly Moeen concedes runs more quickly than all of them. This is partly due to batsmen having changed their approach against spin bowling, which results in runs and wickets coming more quickly, and partly because prolonged accuracy has never been one of his obvious virtues. But look at the names of the spin bowlers behind him on the list: in descending order of wickets taken, they are Lock, Panesar, Titmus, Emburey, Verity, Giles, Rhodes, Edmonds, Allen, Illingworth, Tufnell, Wright, Wardle and Blythe. In that context, how is it that we quibble with Moeen so readily? I suppose it's because we never quite know what's coming.

What is certain is that his spinning colleagues appreciate him hugely. Jack Leach and Dom Bess both speak of his generosity as a senior colleague, even though they are also his rivals. They pool knowledge about bowling at international level and it is Moeen who has the most experience. Actually I'm a fan of all three. Leach has had to overcome so many hurdles in his career; they just keep coming, whether they relate to his health/fitness or his action, and still he perseveres. Nor has Bess's career been straightforward, even though he reached the pinnacle that is international cricket with amazing speed.

I have a few similarities with Bess. We both bowled off breaks that were not reckoned to be international class at Blundell's School in Tiverton, albeit over four decades apart.

We both do as we're told when Mrs Amy Candler speaks – she was one of Dom's teachers and she is my daughter. And I guess we're both pragmatic rather than beautiful batsmen, who should probably score/have scored more runs. Yet there are considerable contrasts as well. Bess is infinitely the better fielder; he takes brilliant catches and conjures run-outs from direct hits, events that decorated my career with the frequency of an appearance by Halley's Comet. He also exhibits much greater confidence in his ability than I managed. He is manifestly up for any challenge. He first impressed the England set-up more with his energy and enthusiasm when participating in the early-morning football and subsequent fielding practice than with the outstanding quality of his off breaks. They immediately liked his 'can-do' attitude and his eagerness to learn and progress. He has already advanced as a bowler; he now propels the ball with more spin and speed and his accuracy is improving.

I was thrilled to give him his first Test cap at Lord's when England were playing Pakistan in May 2018. It is a daunting occasion for the player – and for the person handing over the cap. I got the impression that I might have been more nervous than him. This was the third time I have had the privilege of handing over a cap to a debutant. The first was in Mumbai on 22 December 2012, right at the end of a tour to India. Joe Root was making his T20 debut and everyone else of importance had gone home to prepare for Christmas. So, by process of elimination, I was summoned by the England management to hand over his cap. After my encouragement, I note that England won and Root played a flawless game: he didn't actually have to bat or bowl but he did take a catch in the second over.

At the end of another tour of India – in December 2016 – I gave Hampshire's Liam Dawson his first Test cap. This caused some merriment from Mike Atherton in particular, as he pointed out that in the previous week or two I had been railing in the *Guardian* about England's preference for Dawson ahead of Leach, whom I suggested was a superior bowler. (Unbeknown to us at the time, Leach had been ruled out of contention because of some odd reservations about the validity of his bowling action, which had surfaced after some tests at Loughborough a few months earlier.) Now here I was, doing my best to offer encouragement to Dawson, whom I did not know. In fact, he performed rather well in Chennai – compared to the others. He hit an unbeaten 66 in England's first innings and his figures of 2-129 from 43 overs were rather better, sadly, than those of the other England spinners in the game, Moeen and Adil Rashid. This was the match when England scored 477 in their first innings yet contrived to lose by an innings after India had totted up 759-7 declared. Anyway, it was not Dawson's fault that he had been selected, and I wished him well as best I could.

To hand over that first cap is quite a taxing undertaking but a welcome one for an old player. Obviously it is a great moment for the recipient of the cap and it is therefore important not to spoil it. You have a minute or so to balance congratulations with encouragement without being too pompous or out of touch. Probably best not to open up with the observation that quality finger-spinners were 'ten a penny in my day'. Besides, the role of the finger-spinner has changed a lot since then. I was most successful in one-day cricket at international level. I was accurate rather than penetrative, but batsmen might succumb as they tried to accelerate. Wrist-spinners were deemed a luxury in the short form of the game; unless they were extraordinarily good like Shane Warne, Anil Kumble or Mushtaq Ahmed, they were thought too wayward and not worth the risk. In the twenty-first century the opposite is true: finger-spinners are now often reckoned to be too predictable with a white ball, especially in T20 cricket. The good-length delivery has lost its potency as batsmen – just about any batsman – are confident they can clear the boundary if the ball is 'in the slot'. In the twentieth century, boundary fielders were reliable deterrents to the majority of players. Not any more. So wrist-spinners are deemed essential now; they can create uncertainty since the batsman cannot set himself so early if he does not know which way the ball is going to spin. Moreover, a lack of predictability in line and length can now be regarded as an asset rather than a flaw.

Adil Rashid provides a good example of this trend. He has become one of the best slow bowlers in the world in white-ball cricket. He exudes confidence in these formats now; he remains unperturbed when one of his opponents has cleared the boundary; his googly can befuddle the best and he is not afraid to use it frequently. In Test cricket, he has been England's best wrist-spinner for more than half a century by a huge margin and yet, for all that, his record is modest (he has 60 Test wickets at an average of just under 40).

Now it is the finger-spinner, bolstered by all those DRS lbws, who holds sway in the longest format. All this demonstrates a fascinating evolution of the game. The expectation was that, as games became shorter, the wrist-spinner, especially, would go out of business. But the opposite is true. Meanwhile, the likes of Leach and Bess, both of whom have advanced because of Somerset's decision to produce some turning pitches for Championship cricket, focus on Test selection. In January 2021 in Sri Lanka they played their first Test together and they shared 14 wickets in the match with a few hiccups along the way. Both were short of practice, especially Leach, who for a variety of reasons had not played a Test for fourteen months; in fact, he had barely played any cricket in that time. But in the end they combined well enough. It was reminiscent of this pair playing together at Taunton in recent years (though Bess has now signed for Yorkshire to guarantee a first-team place). The playing surface in Galle was not so different to a few of those at the County Ground in recent times, and gradually these two friends started to feel at home, both revelling in the other's success. England ended up winning the match by seven wickets. There is no doubt that Bess and Leach were enhanced by their experience of bowling together for Somerset in similar conditions – except for the temperature. However, at Taunton they are still awaiting an acknowledgement of the ECB's gratitude for bolstering England's meagre spinning stocks.

5

Declarations

'If I had my time all over again I would
do the same thing.'

Garry Sobers, 1968

DOES ANY OTHER sport have anything like the declaration?
Not that I can think of. In matchplay golf the game can,
theoretically, come to a halt after ten holes if one player has
prevailed on every hole; at the tennis majors a match can last
three sets or five; in boxing someone can be knocked out
in the second minute, but in what other sport can a captain
decide to save time or gain an advantage by shortening the
likely duration of the contest?

The declaration was only allowed after a law change in
1899 and even then it was only permitted on the third day
of the match. It wasn't until 1957 that a declaration was
allowed on the first day. The ability to declare an innings
closed enhances and enlivens the game and is a delicious
addition to the options open to a captain in pursuit of
victory. At least, that is usually the case. The declaration

also has the capacity to provoke argument, intrigue and sometimes anger.

Declarations can be canny – especially when made by Raymond Illingworth – or they can be timid. (There must by now be an algorithm that demonstrates how much time any former captain working as a pundit on radio or television spends pontificating that he would have declared thirty minutes or thirty runs earlier than the blinkered, lily-livered captain out on the field. There may even be another one that demonstrates that the aforementioned, omniscient, cavalier pundit never actually made such an early declaration while he was still playing.) Occasionally declarations can be inspired (inevitably, there is a Mike Brearley example coming up). They can also be 'brave' or 'courageous' – adjectives often used in the manner of Sir Humphrey Appleby of *Yes Minister* fame as terrifying euphemisms. As Sir Humphrey once explained to his increasingly alarmed minister, a 'brave' decision is one that would lose you votes, whereas a 'courageous' one might lose you the election. Of course, we remember the brave/courageous declarations the best. These are the ones that went wrong, and they are especially memorable when they have taken place in a Test match. In county cricket it was once an occupational hazard to lose after a declaration since sides with ambitions to win the Championship put the emphasis on pursuing victory rather than avoiding defeat. But such gambles are rare amid the gravity of a Test match.

The good declarations do not spring to mind so readily, but we should acknowledge one or two. Allan Border, skippering Australia against India at Madras in September 1986, got it right – just about. Australia had dominated the first Test of the series for three days; they posted 574-7 declared after Dean Jones had hit an epic double century despite being hindered by bouts of nausea, fever and leg cramps along the way. When Jones suggested coming off, Border responded with his 'OK, we'll get a Queenslander out there' jibe, which ensured the Victorian Jones kept batting. It seemed certain that India would follow on – in an era when captains usually enforced the follow-on – whereupon Kapil Dev unfurled a brilliant hundred to take the total beyond that target. So Australia batted again and Border declared once more on 170-5 at the end of the fourth day, leaving India to score 348 for victory on the fifth.

Sunil Gavaskar, playing his 100th consecutive Test for India, was still there at tea on the final day when the score was 190-2 with the Australian spinners, Ray Bright and Greg Matthews, bowling the vast majority of the overs. In the last session 158 more runs were required when India decided to go for victory. With five overs left, it looked as if they would get there. At that point India needed 18 runs from 30 balls with four wickets in hand. Then Chetan Sharma was caught on the boundary and the pendulum started swinging again. In the end Ravi Shastri took the single that levelled the scores, but last man Maninder Singh was lbw to the fifth ball of Matthews's over. No wonder Allan Border made a point of praising the Indian umpires at the end of the series, which was drawn. Maninder Singh has always protested that he edged that delivery from Matthews before it hit his pad. But up went the finger.

This was only the second tied Test in history. The first, in 1960 between Australia and the West Indies in Brisbane, contained no dramatic declarations – apart from a few expletives from Australian journalists who had already caught the early flight back to Sydney before the final-session drama unfolded at the Gabba. One man who definitely witnessed both ties is Bobby Simpson. He was opening the batting for Australia in 1960 and coaching them in 1986. Border would recall that Simpson rated the Madras finish as more fascinating because 'we came back from the dead'.

Clearly Gavaskar was a handy man in a run chase. In 1979 at The Oval in the final Test of the summer, Mike Brearley set India 438 to win in what would amount to 151 overs. At one point on the final day, India – brilliantly marshalled by Gavaskar – were 365-1. Then Ian Botham dropped Dilip Vengsarkar on the boundary, a rare event that triggered the young all-rounder into action. Soon he conjured three wickets, a run-out and took a breathtaking catch. One of his victims was Gavaskar, who drilled a catch to mid-on after more than eight hours at the crease during which he had scored 221. Eventually 15 runs were required from the final over, when India were eight wickets down and the match was drawn, but it had needed a Botham intervention and some cunning from Brearley to defy Gavaskar.

That was a conventional declaration, made memorable by an exciting climax. Two years earlier Brearley had made a less conventional declaration in a Championship match between Middlesex and Surrey, which worked even better. Rain had descended upon St John's Wood in the first week of August 1977. By the end of the second of three days, only five overs had been possible and Surrey were 8-1. Maybe the captains could contrive something on the last day. On the third morning, Mike Selvey – Middlesex opening bowler, cricketing sage and lateral thinker – had a look at the playing surface and said to Brearley, 'We could bowl them out twice on here.' Obviously Brearley listened; there were no collaborations between the captains. Instead Middlesex bowled Surrey out for 49 by 12.15 p.m. (Wayne Daniel 5-16, Selvey 3-29, Gatting 2-2.) The expectation was that Middlesex would now glean as many batting points as possible throughout the rest of the day. But then John Emburey and Ian Gould emerged as opening batsmen; Surrey's Robin Jackman bowled one ball, whereupon Brearley declared on 0-0 (at the time it was not possible to forfeit an innings). So Brearley's bowlers set to work again. The unfortunate Monte Lynch registered a pair before lunch and this time Surrey were bowled out for 89. (Daniel 4-23, Selvey 3-31, Gatting 2-1, Emburey 1-17.) Middlesex needed 139 to win and they knocked them off with 11 balls to spare and nine wickets in hand, Brearley 66 not out. At the end of the season Middlesex ended up on the same number of points as Kent at the top of the Championship and the trophy was shared.

It does not always work out like that and such punts are very rare at Test level. It may not have seemed like too much of a gamble when Norman Yardley, England's captain in 1948, set Australia 404 to win on the final day of the Headingley Test. In fact, England had batted on for two overs on that last morning in order to put the heavy roller on the pitch. The idea was that the roller would help to break up the surface, but Don Bradman – who was playing in his penultimate Test match – would later observe that he had never come across a grounds-man who thought the roller ever had this effect. However, by this stage of the match the pitch was bound to offer some turn for the spinners. Bradman gave a short dressing-room speech on that final morning: 'Come on, boys. We can win this match.' But a reminder of Bradman's caginess is evident since we know that before addressing his men he had already instructed the team bus to return to Headingley between lunch and tea. In his diary the night before he had written, 'We are set 400 to win and I fear we may be defeated.' This would have filled him with gloom. Bradman was set upon an invincible tour. His side was 2-0 up in the series and the Ashes had been retained, but he wanted more than that.

For England this was a rare opportunity to beat the Australians. That prospect, along with the knowledge that the great Bradman would never be passing this way again as a player, led to huge queues outside Headingley at dawn. The pitch was worn but who would exploit it for England? Jim Laker was in the team, though not the Laker of 1956, and he was the only specialist spinner. On the first morning, Yardley had had a change of heart when he decided to omit Jack Young, the Middlesex left-arm spinner. How he could have done with him on that final day. Instead Yardley opted to use Denis Compton and, even more surprisingly, Len Hutton, both of whom bowled wrist-spinners – Compton with his left hand, Hutton with his right. Initially Compton caused problems. Even Bradman was struggling to pick him. But that did not apply when Hutton, no doubt a little taken aback to be given the ball, was bowling. In his career Compton would end up with 25 Test wickets (though he took many more for Middlesex) and Hutton with three. Both men were far more capable of winning Test matches for England with their bats than with the ball. Here was an indication of Yardley's desperation to win the game rather than settle for a draw.

On that final day England only took three wickets as Arthur Morris and, inevitably, Bradman pummelled England's bowlers all around Headingley. Compton took 1-82 from 15 overs, Hutton 0-30 from 4 and the more economical Laker was wicketless after 32. Yardley stuck with his spinners come what may. England missed eight or nine chances. Godfrey Evans – behind the stumps on a day when the ball was turning sharply – owned up to having a 'nightmare'. He might have stumped both of Australia's centurions, Morris and Bradman. Rather bewilderingly, he put his errors down to complacency: 'I am afraid we all took our task too lightly. We were all so delighted at being on top before Australia batted that we never really got down to solid concentration.' Complacency against Bradman's Australians? Neil Harvey, 20 years of age, hit the winning boundary and Bradman shouted, 'Come on, son, let's get out of here.' Harvey grabbed a stump and set off in pursuit of his captain. The Australians had won with fifteen minutes and seven wickets to spare, not so much as a result of a bad declaration but because of English ineptitude in the field and, perhaps, in their selection – and because of the brilliance of Bradman and Morris.

Yardley's declaration was not a surprise. If anything, there was mild puzzlement that he should bat for those two overs on the final morning. But the declaration of Garry Sobers two decades later certainly was. The fourth Test in Port of Spain in 1968 appeared to be ambling to yet another draw when Robin Hobbs, the England twelfth man, suddenly appeared on the field soon after lunch on the final day even though no one had summoned him. Colin Cowdrey recalls the moment Hobbs ran up to his captain in his autobiography: '"You had better watch it, skipper," said Hobbs. "The minute you left the pavilion all the West Indians went in and changed into their flannels. It looks as if they are going to declare."'

Agent Hobbs was right. Sobers would explain afterwards that this was a calculated decision rather than a rush of blood from a renowned gambler. He had discussed the plan with the team manager, Everton Weekes, and his teammates. They would set a target of 215 in 165 minutes to win, half-expecting England just to block out for a draw since their tactics had been extremely cautious throughout the series so far. Sobers would write afterwards, 'That series was so boring; the first three Tests had been drawn; England were bowling something like 12 or 13 overs per hour.' He was clearly tired of such negativity. 'I was so fed up. I was there to play cricket and this wasn't what I thought of as cricket. If I had my time all over again I would do the same thing,' he said, a common observation among captains who have declared and lost at Test level. Like Yardley at Headingley, Sobers was banking on his spinners, since he had dropped Wes Hall for this match and Charlie Griffith had suffered an injury early in the game after bowling just three overs. In England's first innings Basil Butcher, an irregular wrist-spinner, had picked up five wickets out of the blue (Cowdrey plus the four tail-enders); also in the side was another wrist-spinner, Willie Rodriguez, as well as Lance Gibbs and Sobers himself.

The grapevine has it that Cowdrey was extremely suspicious of this declaration and had to be persuaded by his senior players, Tom Graveney and Ken Barrington, to go for victory. Unsurprisingly that is not quite how Cowdrey portrays the situation in his autobiography, even if he hints at his own caution: 'It has since been written that there was a dispute in the England dressing room about whether we accepted the challenge and went for these runs or not. There was none. Any caution I had was because I knew there was a tendency in these situations to get over-excited.' However, he adds later: 'Nevertheless, Tom Graveney and Ken Barrington were most reassuring.'

As was the batting of Cowdrey himself and Geoffrey Boycott, the architects of what became a copybook run chase. England won by seven wickets with three minutes to spare, Cowdrey scoring a polished 71, Boycott a superbly judged, unbeaten 80. 'That declaration and result followed me for the remainder of my career,' wrote Sobers, who was forever diminished as a captain by this loss. 'Clive Lloyd has always been called the West Indies' greatest ever captain, yet Clive declared in Trinidad leaving India over 400 to win and lost with 15 minutes to spare. I left a target of 215 and didn't have fast bowlers. Which is worse?' asked Sobers. Clearly this match left some sizeable scars in the Caribbean.

Clive Lloyd was the youngster in the West Indies team in 1968; by 1976 he was indisputably the captain. His side had won the first ever World Cup final at Lord's, in 1975, and was soon to assert its dominance in Test cricket. But they encountered some problems against India in April 1976 in a series in the Caribbean that helped to forge the template that ensured they became the best side in the world for over a decade. The West Indies won the first Test of a four-match series emphatically in Barbados, with Viv Richards – now in full blossom – and Lloyd hitting centuries. In Port of Spain, India would have won the second Test but they missed chances galore in the field and the home side survived. The third match was supposed to be played in Guyana but, as rain kept descending upon Georgetown, it was switched back to Port of Spain. With Richards to the fore again, striking 177 out of a total of 359, the West Indies dominated. By mid-afternoon on the fourth day, Lloyd declared with a lead of 402. At this point in history only Bradman's Australians at Headingley had successfully chased a target in excess of 400 in Test cricket. This was the match Sobers was referring to in his defence.

Yet again Sunil Gavaskar played a key role in the fourth innings of a Test match. He hit another polished century, while his brother-in law, Gundappa Viswanath, sparkled in the second half of the run chase. India won with the loss of just four wickets, and two of those were from run-outs. Take a look at the West Indies line-up: there was a young Michael Holding, who took six wickets in the first innings, the left-handed swing bowler Bernard Julien, and three slow bowlers, the wrist-spinner Imtiaz Ali (in his solitary Test), the off-spinner Albert Padmore (in the first of his two Tests) and the orthodox left-armer Raphick Jumadeen. Andy Roberts had been omitted due to exhaustion after an unrelenting eighteen months on the road.

Upon reflection and after the passage of quite a lot of time, Lloyd was more prepared than Sobers – and most other losing captains after an unsuccessful declaration – to acknowledge that mistakes had been made. 'We had this stupid notion that spinners would get people out in Trinidad,' he recalled. 'And they've never done so. That's not to say that there wasn't turn at Queen's Park – there was – but it turned slowly. Yet the mythical connection between spinners and Trinidad [which may have prompted Sobers' declaration back in 1968] remained.' This result prompted Lloyd to change tack – decisively. 'I wasn't against spinners. If I'd had a Shane Warne he would have played every day. I thought Jumadeen was pretty good. We thought for a while that Padmore might replace Lance [Gibbs]. They were given a chance but the point is that they did not win matches for us. Our fast bowlers were the ones winning matches.'

The next Test was in Jamaica. Imtiaz Ali and Padmore were dropped; in came Vanburn Holder, dependable though not an express bowler, and the young Wayne Daniel, an express bowler who was not yet dependable since this was his debut. Daniel was only 20 and I already knew about him. In August 1974 I had played against him, which had been a bit of a shock to the system. The West Indies Young Cricketers toured the UK that summer and I represented England, which may surprise you a little, as a specialist batsman, which may surprise you a lot. I batted at four with a young Chris Cowdrey at five and Mike Gatting at six. At this stage in my career there was little danger of my being asked to bowl. Daniel had not played in the previous game at Arundel, where we had noted that the West Indies had a classy batsman in Jeffrey Dujon (he did not keep wicket in that match) and a disciplined but unremarkable bowling attack (i.e. there was no one especially quick). But then we saw Daniel – already a magnificent physical specimen – at the end of his run-up and we soon reached the conclusion that he propelled the ball faster than any of us had seen before.

To say that Daniel's bowling was something of an eye-opener is an understatement. This was uncharted territory. There were no helmets available – they had yet to be developed – so we plonked our new caps on our heads with pride but also the vain hope that they might somehow offer protection if we were hit by one of Daniel's howitzers. Would we be able to see the ball? There were no guarantees of that. It was probably worse waiting to find out than being at the crease. In the middle, most of us began to discover that the ball was just about visible; Daniel had the grace to have a good clean seeing action and the decency to sweat a lot. At least he gave the impression that he had to work hard to bowl fast. With his legs already pumping like mighty pistons, he accelerated up to the crease, leapt high and hurled the ball down as fast as he could. This was a brief but harsh introduction to what the real world would be like as a professional cricketer. Fear was most definitely a factor. None of us who faced him in 1974 was surprised to see him in the West Indies team in 1976. In fact, it cheered us up a bit because our initial impression was that he was rather special. Quite how he ended up playing only ten Tests for the West Indies is a bit of a mystery as well as confirmation of the incredible conveyor belt of pacemen in the Caribbean in this era.

The playing surface at Sabina Park in Daniel's first Test match was unreliable, the bounce at one end being especially untrustworthy. Even so, at the end of a shortened first day India were 178-1 despite Anshuman Gaekwad taking several blows on the body. On the second morning, Holding struck with the new ball, having Viswanath caught at backward short leg off the glove with the impact fracturing his finger. Brijesh Patel edged a delivery from Vanburn Holder on to his mouth and Gaekwad was struck just above the left ear when ducking against Holding. Once India had reached 306-6, Bishan Bedi declared but his decision was not triggered by the strength of his side's position. Two men had retired hurt and Bedi decided that neither he nor Bhagwat Chandrasekhar – the team's key bowler and a hopeless batsman – would risk injury by going out to bat.

Wisden records that there was a surfeit of short-pitched bowling, with Holding sometimes operating from around the wicket to make evasion even more difficult for the batsmen, but the correspondent also notes the increasing unpredictability of the bounce. West Indies scored 391 in reply and India's second innings soon faltered to the point that they were 97-5, whereupon Bedi called his batsmen in with a lead of 12. Obviously the assumption was that Bedi had declared but after the match he insisted the innings should be recorded as being completed. Three men were absent hurt, while Bedi and Chandrasekhar once again declined to come out to bat. Recalling the game years later, Lloyd said that he was annoyed at the way the game ended. 'Gaekwad in the first innings showed when he got 80-odd that if you're brave enough you'll make runs. This is Test cricket, you know. As for the bowling, my memory is that there was a ridge at one end – I think they had trouble with an underground pipe that raised up the earth – so the ball took off when it hit that ridge. That pitch and the one at Old Trafford later in the year [when the West Indies were accused of bowling an excess of short-pitched deliveries especially when John Edrich and Brian Close were at the crease] were the two worst I saw in my Test career. But you play the game. Any talk of intimidatory bowling is false – a false accusation.'

But how do you define intimidatory bowling? I think we can safely conclude that Bedi and Chandrasekhar, who was a famously inept tail-ender, were intimidated, just as Lance Gibbs had been on the West Indies tour to Australia a few months earlier against Dennis Lillee and Jeff Thomson. The game was changing fast. Lloyd drew another conclusion. From now on, he would not bother with a gaggle of moderate spinners in his side whatever the conditions; he would rely on his fast men instead. Moreover, the tacit understanding among old fast bowlers, which meant that pacemen never bounced fellow tail-enders, was fast disappearing. This was a ruthless game that made the advent of the helmet more urgent. And nothing has changed since then. On England's last Ashes tour in 2017/18 their tail-enders received nothing but short-pitched deliveries from an exceptional Australian pace attack, and no one including the umpires batted an eyelid. It was an ugly sight, demanding an intervention, but now this was deemed to be the norm. There were no complaints from England; to do so would have constituted Pommie whingeing.

Such bowling was not the norm back in 1976. Bedi and Gavaskar were incensed at the tactics employed by the West Indies and by the behaviour of the home crowd. Gavaskar recalls being in his stance against Holding and Daniel and constantly hearing the chants of 'Kill him, kill him.' In his autobiography, *Sunny Days*, he wrote about the hostility of the crowd in terms that would never have been permitted by the editors of this era. In a chapter entitled 'Barbarism in Kingston' Gavaskar tells of the reaction in the stands to Gaekwad being hit: 'They were stamping their legs, clapping and jumping with joy. The only word I can think of to describe the behaviour of the crowd is "barbarian". Here was a man seriously injured, and these barbarians were thirsting for more blood, instead of expressing sympathy, as any civilized and sporting crowd would have done... The whole thing was sickening. Never have I seen such cold-blooded and positively indifferent behaviour from cricket officials. And the spectators, to put it mildly, were positively inhuman.' Upon his arrival home, Bedi would say that 'the West Indies tactics in this game were not part of cricket' and he could point to the sight of his heavily bandaged trio of batsmen returning to Indian soil as evidence.

Our next declaration also involved the West Indies and once again they were the beneficiaries rather than the perpetrators. This one was made by David Gower at Lord's in 1984 and, as with Yardley in 1948, there was a bit of mumbling and grumbling – even from the chairman of selectors, Peter May – that the England captain had left it too long before declaring. The situation was similar to 1948. England were being outplayed by a vastly superior side but at last they had found themselves in a strong position by the fourth evening, when Allan Lamb and Derek Pringle were batting. The lead was over 300 and the light was deteriorating to such an extent that the umpires offered the batsmen the option of going off. Lamb and Pringle looked to the Pavilion for guidance, but no such guidance was forthcoming; there was no sign of captain Gower on the England balcony. At the time Gower probably mumbled an explanation along the lines of 'it's up to the guys out there to decide if they can see the ball properly', but in both of his autobiographies he acknowledges that he was, in fact, watching the tennis on the TV in the dressing room when his batsmen were seeking direction from him. 'Had they known I was sitting inside watching Wimbledon I dread to think what they might have written.'

In fact Gower was given more stick for his absence from the balcony than for his declaration. In his first autobiography (1992) he says, 'I thought we were fairly well insured against defeat but I had not bargained for us bowling total crap.' In his second (2013) he may have mellowed a bit in his assessment of his bowlers, pointing out how the flat pitch and clear skies had delayed his declaration longer than May would have liked and that Gordon Greenidge played 'an extraordinary innings'. In the West Indies' first innings Ian Botham had taken 8-103, but there was no magic on tap in the second. After 66.1 overs West Indies were 344-1, Greenidge unbeaten on 214 and the game was won. Desmond Haynes was the solitary batsman dismissed and that was from a run-out. There were still eleven more overs available when West Indies reached their target. 'At least we got them to the final hour,' Gower later observed.

So he became the second England captain to declare in the third innings of a Test match and to lose the game. There are two more to come. Just one Australian has achieved this feat (they are not quite so gung-ho as they make out down there), and he was not a regular captain. In 2001 Adam Gilchrist, frustrated by the intervention of rain, made a generous declaration at Headingley, where strange things happen. The series was already won and the Australians craved a clean sweep, but they reckoned without a brilliant innings from Mark Butcher. The target ended up as 311 from 90 overs as the Australians pursued a 'greenwash'. After the early loss of Mike Atherton and Marcus Trescothick, Butcher cracked an unbeaten 173 and the game was won with 20 overs to spare. The Aussies shrugged their shoulders, shook Butcher by the hand, and then normal service was resumed when captain Steve Waugh returned from injury at The Oval, where the tourists won the final Test by an innings and 25 runs.

Sometimes declarations can be controversial without the match being lost. This was the case with Rahul Dravid in 2004 and Mike Atherton in 1995. Dravid in particular is not a man to court controversy, but in Multan against Pakistan he managed to cause quite a stir. India were piling on the runs.

Virender Sehwag hit a triple century but – with India 675-5 and Sachin Tendulkar on 194 not out – Dravid, standing in for the injured Sourav Ganguly, declared. Despite their dominance over their great rivals, once Tendulkar let it be known that he 'felt let down' by the declaration so close to a double century, India 'had a hot potato on our hands' (to use the phrase of their coach, John Wright). Tendulkar did not come out to field on that second evening, claiming a sprained ankle, but he was fit enough to express his surprise and disappointment at Dravid's declaration after the close of play.

This controversy contrived to overshadow India's first ever win in Pakistan, and surprisingly Tendulkar would only score 11 more runs in three innings during a run-drenched series, which was eventually won 2-1 by India. They like their landmarks in the subcontinent and this declaration sparked an angry debate throughout the nation. Had Tendulkar been robbed by the nefarious Dravid, the least likely villain in the cricketing firmament, or was India's greatest batsman obsessed by personal milestones? There was a theory that in India a milestone was almost as important as a victory; on the 1984/85 tour we reckoned that an Indian batsman approaching a century in an ODI match was almost certain to become more cautious and to proceed more slowly. Here was one reason to bowl first, since any such batsman approaching three figures would not be hindered by a victory target.

Ganguly, the injured captain looking on, may have been frustrated that Tendulkar was not accelerating appropriately; Wright, the coach, had advocated an earlier declaration to

Dravid, which would have avoided the issue. No batsman can complain about a declaration when he is on 170. But it was Dravid who made the declaration after Yuvraj Singh's dismissal. There were hasty late-night, clear-the-air meetings. There had been communication cock-ups, perhaps, but no conspiracies. Tendulkar was quietly fuming; that night he took to his headphones and to the gym to work out his frustrations (as we learn from the five pages devoted to this incident in his autobiography). From this distance the hubbub does not reflect that well on Tendulkar but, in his favour, he did not pretend that the denial of another double century was of no consequence to him; he was angry but he tells us that no long-term damage was done to the relationships of those involved.

Something similar – but not the same – had happened a decade earlier when the pursuit of an important milestone also hindered the captain's declaration plans. England, led by Mike Atherton, were in Sydney for the New Year Test of 1995. The series was still alive as this was only the third Test of the series. England were already trailing 2-0 but they had dominated this match, and on the fourth afternoon Atherton was contemplating his declaration. He was eager to bowl at Australia before tea to allow his pacemen two chances with the new ball on either side of the interval. The problem was that Graeme Hick was nearing what could become his third Test century and, perhaps more significantly, his first against Australia. But with the lead nearing 450, he was dawdling. On 98 Hick blocked three successive deliveries and Atherton lost patience and declared. At the time my sympathies were with Atherton. The Ashes were still alive – just – and there was a game to be won; there was no more time to waste and there was rain around.

Now, like Atherton, I think the declaration was a mistake, even though the match was ultimately drawn. In cricketing terms it was wholly justified; England needed to be out there and bowling. But the incident clearly disheartened the tour party. Cricketers feed off landmarks and this is not always an entirely selfish thing. Goals can be a spur and perhaps the best example comes from Sir Richard Hadlee, who was motivated by the pursuit of carefully calculated statistical targets. Hick, unlike Tendulkar in Multan, needed a confidence boost. Tendulkar was the best player in the world and everyone knew it. Hick – partly because of his staggering start in county cricket – was already labelled an under-achiever and, in the biting words of John Bracewell, a 'flat-track bully'. A century against Australia would help to counteract those assessments. He should have gone faster at the end of England's innings, but Atherton should have indulged him. In the long term that might have been beneficial for Hick and England. Like Tendulkar, Hick was fuming; unlike Tendulkar, he was reluctant to discuss the matter with his captain. 'He took it badly,' recalled Atherton. 'He didn't speak to me for the rest of the day, nor would he throw the ball to me in the field. That evening I went to his room to try to smooth things out but the hurt on his face was plain to see and he refused to allow me to heal the rift. He barely spoke to me for the rest of the tour.' In the event, a prolapsed disc forced Hick to leave that Ashes tour prematurely.

Now to a declaration that was widely applauded at the time, though not by me. Adelaide 2006 and England, led by Andrew Flintoff, were 1-0 down in the series. But by the third session of the second day, having won the toss, they were still batting and the score was in excess of 500. Kevin Pietersen and Paul Collingwood had added 310 together. Heady times on an Ashes tour. Around about this time I was asked to join Mark Pougatch on Radio 5 Live for some sort of update for startled early-morning listeners in the UK. He asked me about the timing of any declaration. I remember expressing the view that England should keep batting, grinding their formidable opponents into the dust – though by now, after long periods of turgid cricket from the noble Collingwood, they were racing along nicely with captain Flintoff at the helm. This was such a rare opportunity to turn the tables on their great tormentors, McGrath and Warne.

Soon after I put down the microphone, Flintoff declared on 551-5. My heart sank, and not just because this declaration seemed to make my sage observations on the radio look a bit silly. Whatever cricketing instincts I possessed were telling me this was a bad declaration. England had nine overs to bowl that evening and during that time Matthew Hoggard removed Justin Langer so that Australia were 28-1 at the close. Those chastising me for being such a negative curmudgeon were swift to point out the benefit of the declaration as England had snatched an important wicket late in the day. But my gut instincts did not allow me to concede the point. When Flintoff walked back to the dressing room that evening, Shane Warne was at his mercy. He had bowled 53 overs and taken 1-167; McGrath had figures of 0-107 from 30 overs. This was unprecedented territory for English batsmen. Here was an opportunity to inflict further punishment and maybe even to trigger some self-doubt among the two giants, who were obviously coming to the end of their careers. Bat on, please, bat on. Both Warne and McGrath were on the ropes so keep pummelling them. Had I been more alert, I might also have pointed out that Australia had scored 556 against India at this venue three years earlier – and yet they lost the game.

You probably know what happened next. I'll spare the Poms out there the gory minutiae of the disintegration of the England batsmen in their second innings. As for the Aussies, I'm sure you know every twist and turn far better than the words of 'Advance Australia Fair'. This would become Australia's Headingley '81, a match that could not possibly be lost by the tourists – until that miraculous turnaround on the final day. It was slow torture as it became apparent that the England dressing room was suddenly so fearful of an unthinkable defeat that gradually became an inevitability. Despite my reservations on that second day, even I had not seriously considered the possibility of England losing at the end of play on the fourth evening. By then England were 59-1 from 19 overs in their second innings, a lead of 97. 'This game is going nowhere,' I told my readers before contemplating the possible decline of the great McGrath. As it turned out, the game was going into a dark abyss from which the England touring party would never escape on that tour. Warne and McGrath took 1-267 from 83 overs in the first innings, 6-64 from 42 overs in the second, and Australia won by six wickets.

I promised you the two other England captains to have declared in the third innings of a Test before losing the game. They are Kevin Pietersen in Chennai in December 2008 and Joe Root at Headingley, yet again, in 2017. England's defeat after India had been set 387 for victory in what was supposed to be 126 overs (a slow over rate meant England would never have bowled that many, and in the end only 98.3 were needed) does not figure prominently in the Pietersen autobiography. Recalling that expedition, he notes that Sachin Tendulkar played 'a remarkable innings' in Chennai and 'I got a hundred in the second Test but we lost the series.' That, he – or his ghostwriter – decided, would be enough about the cricket on Pietersen's solitary winter as England's captain. Well, he had some distractions, I suppose. He already knew his relationship with coach Peter Moores was doomed to failure and, after a stream of defeats in ODI cricket in India, the Test series had been thrown into serious doubt after the Mumbai bombings at the Taj Mahal Hotel, for years England's chosen resting place in the city. As captain, Pietersen had been heavily involved in the negotiations to enable the series to continue. In the wake of the bombings the players had returned home but within a few days Pietersen had advocated a return to India even though some of his players were reluctant. Here was Pietersen the diplomat. I can remember him being very cooperative, crouching in the media bus, to give a press conference to the English press just before that first Test in Chennai. He seemed to be saying

– and doing – all the right things in a very tense situation. If at all possible the show must go on and all India would be grateful to Pietersen – and his team.

The Test match, conducted amid 'presidential' security, unfolded dramatically. As it happens, two of KP's future adversaries will remember it with more enthusiasm. Andrew Strauss hit two centuries; Graeme Swann made his Test debut and took two wickets in his first over. It was a terrific game. On the fourth afternoon the Pietersen declaration, which now sounds like a Robert Ludlum blockbuster, made sense. England were nine down at the time so there may not have been many more runs forthcoming anyway. However, Virender Sehwag soon made a mockery of it. In that evening session Sehwag shredded the England attack, cracking 83 from 68 balls – he was the one who played a 'remarkable innings' – so that India only required 256 more runs to win on the final day. The pitch declined to deteriorate and England did not bowl very well. The general view was 'magnificent match, cricket was the winner in the aftermath of tragedy, and England – under the leadership of Pietersen – had done everyone a good turn simply by turning up' – rather like John Pullin's England rugby players in Dublin in 1973.

The second Test was in Chandigarh, a venue that India often go to when there are security issues. There were a lot of runs, a lot of fog and a lot of bad light. The trip from the hotel to the ground – amid more extensive security – was always an eerie experience as the fog rolled around the makeshift dwellings en route. Impoverished, scantily clad young kids would be washing themselves in the cool, clawing morning mist while clutching their mobile phones. The match, Pietersen's last as captain of England, was doomed to be a draw. His century was one of his few forgettable ones.

Pietersen's declaration in Chennai was rather better than Joe Root's at Headingley against the West Indies in 2017, though no one mentioned that at the time. Root received no castigation for his declaration – he set the West Indies 322 to win in what would have been 96 overs. Shai Hope, amazingly, became the first man to score two hundreds in the same match at Headingley. This landmark had been beyond Donald Bradman, Herbert Sutcliffe, Len Hutton and Geoffrey Boycott, but not Hope. At the time of writing, Hope has only ever hit two Test hundreds – in thirty-four matches and sixty-four innings – so Root may consider himself a bit unlucky. Yet he escaped criticism of his declaration mainly because the pundits had all gone out of their way to praise such a 'positive' move on the fourth evening. They could hardly castigate him twenty-four hours later, although we all know that the sages beyond the boundary can change their opinions rapidly and brazenly without too many remembering their U-turns. It is different for those with real responsibility. At the very least Root was taking a lot for granted when he declared. He certainly underestimated his opponents. Given that England had won the previous match – a horrendous affair at Edgbaston that is likely to remain as the solitary day/night Test ever played in England – by an innings and 209 runs, this is not so surprising. However, the old notion of keeping the opposition 'interested' in a run chase so that they might forfeit some wickets late in their innings seldom applies now. Most modern batsmen do not like batting for a draw and many are inept at doing so, though this may not apply to the West Indies' other batting hero in this Test, Kraigg Brathwaite. So Root joined Norman Yardley (1948) and Adam Gilchrist (2001) in Headingley declaration folklore. I'm pretty sure he also expressed 'no regrets' afterwards, but he has since been a bit cagier with his declarations. In Chennai in February 2021 Root received routine flak from the pundits for not declaring on the fourth evening and England won with three hours to spare.

Most of the above are essentially innocent cock-ups. One or two declarations go beyond that. I have already written, in *Original Spin*, about Brian Rose's declaration when captain of Somerset in a zonal B&H match in 1978 at Worcester. He left the crease with his opening partner after one over with the score at 1-0. Somerset lost the match by ten wickets but mathematically were assured of their place in the quarter-finals. In fact, they were thrown out of the competition, so I think this qualifies for the 'poor declaration' column. It was a bad decision which betrayed his desperation to lead Somerset to a trophy for the first time. 'It only took a few days' reflection for me to realise that what I had done was wrong, certainly in the context of the spirit of the game, and the barrage of criticism hurt,' wrote Brian in his autobiography. However, this declaration somehow increased the resolve of that Somerset side, binding them together, and it prompted a rule change: declarations were not to be allowed in one-day matches thereafter.

There was a more pernicious declaration at Centurion

Park in South Africa in 2000, which was highly praised at the time. After three days of rain and with the series already won, South Africa's captain, Hansie Cronje, suggested they should have a game with England, which meant forfeiting two innings. He made Nasser Hussain an offer that could hardly be refused. Having been alerted that Cronje was keen for some negotiations, Hussain had been expecting a target of 300 or more and he had expected some haggling, which was always the way when Keith Fletcher at Essex was operating so cunningly in the County Championship. So Hussain said 250 and remarkably Cronje said, 'OK.' Also in the room was Phil Tufnell (not playing in that game), who was gobsmacked by the deal, much more so than his captain who, admittedly, had more on his mind.

So Cronje declared on 248-8 and after those forfeitures England had 76 overs to try to get those runs. England won by two wickets. In the immediate aftermath Hussain, elated by his second Test victory as captain, said, 'I hope Hansie gets the credit he deserves,' an assessment that had to be amended a few months later. To do the deal and get the leather jacket as well as 53,000 rand (about £5000 at the time), Cronje had to ensure the match was not drawn. At the time Atherton's guts, like Tufnell's, told him something was wrong here – 'for the first time in my life I felt completely flat at the moment of a Test victory'. But the following weekend most of us wrote of Cronje as a knight in shining armour, selflessly resurrecting a dead match for the greater good. I certainly did, just as most of us lauded the appointment of Salman Butt as Pakistan's new, urbane Test captain in 2010 – a young man who would surely be a steady hand on the tiller of Pakistan cricket for years to come.

Another declaration that did not work out perfectly was made by Carew Cricket Club in Pembrokeshire at the end of the 2017 season. The idea was that, by declaring on 18-1, they would ensure they won Pembroke CCC's Division One ahead of nearby rivals, Cresselly. Andy Bull, who is forever finding sources of fascination from unlikely places for the *Guardian*, outlined the situation neatly.

> Carew were 21 points ahead. Under the league rules, a team gets 20 points for a win, plus whatever bonuses they earn along the way. The batting side get one bonus point for the first 40 runs they make, another for every other 40 runs, until they reach 200 runs. The bowling team gets a bonus point for every two wickets they take. So Cresselly didn't just need to win, they had to score two more bonus points than Carew too. And if Carew scored so many as 10 points, they'd win the league. Which, Cresselly say, is why they chose to bowl when they won the toss. After 15 balls, Carew were 18 for 1. And then they declared. Which made it very easy for Cresselly to get 20 points, but impossible for them to get 21.

Well, this ploy worked a bit better than Brian Rose's but it was not entirely successful. A four-man disciplinary committee was hastily convened and they decided that Carew CC would remain as champions but they would also be relegated. I see that they won Division Two in 2018 and so they were promoted back to Division One at the first attempt. In 2019 they finished fourth in Division One, one place behind Cresselly. But had that declaration at the end of the 2017 season really been worthwhile? Of course not.

6

Crowds

'Leave our flies alone.'

Stephen Harold Gascoigne, Sydney 1933

PEERING OUT OF my hotel room, the great white pylons of the Melbourne Cricket Ground, no more than a hundred yards away, invaded the skyline beyond the Hilton Hotel, a constant reminder of the trials to come. The MCG was a twentieth-century Colosseum. And, having recently flown in from India, the England cricket team were the Christians.

We had been in India for four months in the winter of 1984/85 on a traumatic tour and an unforgettable one, which had coincided with the assassinations of the Prime Minister, Mrs Gandhi, and the Deputy British High Commissioner, Percy Norris, as well as the Bhopal disaster and a general election. Against this febrile backdrop, David Gower's team had stayed on and won the Test series 2-1, despite losing the first match in Bombay, and the ODI series 4-1. Then the squad left India – not for a bit of respite back home but for Australia to play in what was modestly billed as 'The Greatest Show on Earth' in Victoria and New South Wales. We went there for the World Championship of Cricket, a quick-fire one-day series with all the Test-playing nations competing. The winners would be... actually you'll have to hang on a bit because I've no idea – except I know it wasn't England – and I'll have to look it up... India.

The state of Victoria was celebrating its 150th anniversary and the centrepiece was to be a cricket match between England and Australia in Melbourne, where those massive new pylons now sprouted state-of-the-art floodlights that would soon become a familiar landmark on the city's skyline. Night cricket, first introduced by Kerry Packer, had been a feature at the Sydney Cricket Ground for several years, but now the MCG would be able to boast bigger and better lights. Every seat was sold – approximately 85,000 of them – and how better to start the celebrations than by humbling a few weary Poms?

There was no shortage of pomp and ceremony. The teams were paraded around the ground as if this were the start of the Olympic Games, dutifully smiling and waving even as we made our way past Bay 13, from where the spectators responded with a stream of abuse at their visitors, just to assert their bona fide Aussie credentials. I made a note of that. There was nothing as sophisticated as the exhortation to Douglas Jardine on the Bodyline tour. 'Leave our flies alone. They are your only friends here,' memorably sprang from the lips of Stephen Harold Gascoigne – aka Yabba – the famous barracker who always encamped on the hill at the SCG. Instead there was just undiluted, unsavoury, unfunny abuse.

Finally we were ushered to the podium at the other end of the ground in front of the members' stand. The state premier, John Cain, tried to make a speech but was soon overwhelmed by chants of 'Boring, boring'. Up next was Bob Hawke, a more experienced politician and the prime minister, who won himself a bit of time by describing the Victorians as 'the most knowledgeable and discerning cricketing public in the world', after which he had the wisdom not to hang around. Soon he declared this great tournament was under way, whereupon the brass band hammered out 'Waltzing Matilda' and 'Advance Australia Fair'. Hawke tossed a specially minted coin into the air and our captain, David Gower, unsure how effective these new lights would be, won the toss and decided to bat before darkness descended.

The odds were always against us. The tour of India had been something of a triumph. To general surprise, despite such a volatile situation, the trip proceeded and somehow England's callow squad had prevailed. It had been the most arduous, memorable and rewarding of expeditions. But, after four months on the road, we were exhausted. Upon arrival in Sydney, where everything suddenly seemed so fresh and clear, where the wine and beer were like nectar, we relaxed a bit and it was tricky to regain the sense of purpose that had been so evident in India. We did our best to go back to the well but there was nothing there.

At the MCG the dressing room was a long way from the middle; in fact, everything was a long way from the middle at the biggest cricket ground in the world. Up the stairs was a viewing area but the dressing room was subterranean, which allowed no sight of the cricket going on outside. Our innings started well enough, faltered and then recovered via Allan Lamb and Mike Gatting to the point where we were 159-3. Then we were suddenly 159-5 with both our key batsmen gone. I missed the second dismissal since I was downstairs, strapping on my pads and searching for my helmet. A voice from above alerted me to the fact that it was my turn now. I just about avoided the nightmarish scenario that disturbs so many cricketers before dawn: pads strapped on in the nick of time but no boots on my feet and no bat anywhere to be seen as the clock ticks away.

It was a long trek out to the middle, which at least offered a chance to adjust to the light and the noise. The spectators were finding their voice, and the Aussie bowlers – themselves a bit jaded after a long summer – had more of a spring in their step. Chris Cowdrey fell straightaway, lbw to his first delivery from Craig McDermott: 166-6. So, rather laboriously, Phil Edmonds and I set about restoring the situation.

I don't remember much about this mini-recovery – and it was only a mini-recovery. We crept to 214-8 from our allotted overs in the end. It was noisy out there but it was still light and therefore not so unusual. My experience of batting under lights two years earlier had been more memorable, though no more successful. At the SCG in January 1983 in my first ever floodlit match England had bowled Australia out for 180, with Geoff Miller and I sharing five cheap wickets; at the halfway point we seemed favourites to win but it was not to be. That night in Sydney the Australians rallied with some vigour within and beyond the boundary. The crescendo of invisible sound as they turned the tables was beyond anything I had experienced on a cricket field. The cacophony seemed to be coming from nowhere because I could not see the crowd; I just heard them rejoicing at Australia's comeback. I joined Miller in the middle and we could barely hear each other speak during our mid-wicket conference, and it was downright impossible to hear one another calling – not that we ran between the wickets very often.

It must have been great theatre for the home crowd. Rodney Hogg, a streaky pace bowler, was clearly galvanized by the occasion and he was bowling fast. As he followed through I could see his eyes popping out of his head yet still staring at me as I rubbed the inside of my thigh. He may have said something but still I could not hear a word. Our innings petered out tamely and we lost by 31 runs. *Wisden* records that 'England batted poorly in front of a large, loud and partisan crowd.' No arguments there. I remember being not out at the end; I had forgotten (but have just checked) that I had been out there for three-quarters of an hour, facing 36 balls for just seven runs. But I have never forgotten the noise or those eyes on stalks, which belonged to such a genial man – off the pitch.

A couple of years later, as we made our way out to defend our modest total at Melbourne with the lights on and the sun disappearing, I used a bit of experience. I knew I would probably be required to field at mid-on and then third man, the standard shift for an ordinary fielder, and so I made an innocent-looking beeline for the members' end at the MCG. This left Jonathan Agnew – unusually behind the game – with little alternative but to be stationed at the other end in front of

Bay 13. This was quite an eye-opener for our sensitive nasty fastie. He later reported that he was subjected to constant, mindless, vicious abuse down there – good practice for the Twitter era, I suppose – which was probably not such a great surprise to him. But he was taken aback to be flashed repeatedly by a spectator down on the boundary edge. The vitriol that emanated from Bay 13 became legendary and was often a source of much amusement. But now it seems more barbaric, especially since I'm writing this soon after the Sydney Test between Australia and India in January 2021, during which Indian cricketers on the boundary were racially abused by spectators who were eventually removed from the ground. Progress? What progress?

By contrast, back in 1985 it was really quite civilized in front of the members' stand. Australia started well in their run chase but were reduced to 58-3 after Allan Border had swept my first delivery into the hands of Norman Cowans at deep backward square leg. Thereafter, Dean Jones and Robbie Kerr restored the situation all too easily. There was an eerie atmosphere out in the middle; it was obviously noisy with constant cheering and jeering from the stands, yet around the square itself there was a strange silence. I could hear none of the usual bellows of encouragement from sergeant major Gatting or wicketkeeper Downton as they were drowned out by the background noise. So we were all operating in our little world, with no possible connection to our teammates unless they were standing no more than a yard away. Phil Edmonds, in particular, was hyped up. When he was bowling, his aggression was not only directed at the Australian batsmen; he yelled abuse at erring fieldsmen on his own side with the same venom but fortunately we could hear nothing. We lost by seven wickets.

The MCG is a great ground when it is full. It is a strange place to play when it's empty. I was back there in January 1987 when there were approximately 84,800 fewer spectators in the stadium. On this occasion I was playing for Western Australia against Victoria in the Sheffield Shield. It was an earnest enough contest and in some ways a forerunner to the experience imposed on our cricketers during lockdown in 2020. On this occasion every comment from a stray spectator echoed around the vast concrete bowl. I recall our twelfth man coming on as a sub, a young clubmate of mine from Perth, called Gary Ireland, who was a fine batsman and about 5 feet 4 inches tall. After fielding for an over, he returned to the pavilion and a lone voice bellowed and echoed around the stands: 'Ah, come on, let the little kid have a bit more of a run around.'

If nothing else, this confirmed an incontrovertible truth that applies as much today as it did then: that far more people come to watch domestic first-class cricket in England than anywhere else in the world. When WA were playing in Perth during that season the crowd would never reach four figures, even though everyone in the city might be following our progress towards winning the Shield. Aaron Finch made this point neatly when he came to England as captain of Australia's white-ball side in the summer of 2020. He was asked about playing in empty stadiums and replied that it should not be too much of a problem since 'most of us have spent 95 per cent of our cricketing lives playing in front of nobody'. This certainly applied in grade cricket in Australia as well as Shield matches; in my first game of club cricket in Perth in 1981 arguably the greatest Australian fast bowler of all time, Dennis Lillee, was in the opposition. To my surprise, nobody apart from the odd relative of the players involved was there to watch him.

Maybe this helps to explain the remarkable intensity of the recent matches played behind closed doors. The cricketers were just drawing upon their early experiences when they were accustomed to operating in a vacuum. Even when a crowd is in attendance, the professional is often capable of cutting himself off and concentrating on his own game, although – as Agnew discovered in Melbourne – that is not so easy in hostile territory.

Wisely, Agnew did not take the matter into his own hands at the MCG. It would not have been a good idea for him to waltz into the stands to confront his Bay 13 tormentor and, however outraged, I'm pretty sure he did not consider this option. But this is what Inzamam ul-Haq famously did at a most unlikely venue – the Toronto Cricket, Skating and Curling Club – in 1997. Pakistan were playing a one-day match there against India. Inzamam was fielding on the boundary and was subjected to constant abuse. (The translation archly suggests that he was being called 'a rotten potato'.) He had had enough, so he asked the twelfth man to bring him his bat – a request that was swiftly granted – and, armed with this treasured weapon, he went into the stands to seek out whoever was abusing him. The bat did not actually make contact with anyone, but Inzamam's intent was clear; he was banned for two ODIs.

Nor did the bat of Viv Richards cause any damage as he was leaving the field in Yorkshire, at decorous Harrogate rather than down-to-earth Headingley, in 1975. 'Hurry up, you black bastard,' shouted one of the spectators. Viv had been nursing an ankle injury but he moved fast enough now – towards the offending group of spectators. 'Whoever said that can get up,' he said. Afterwards he recalled, 'No one did. They never do. I accept that it was an ugly incident. I must have held that bat menacingly and my eyes blazed. But I don't think I did anything wrong.' He never heard anything from Yorkshire about the incident.

Such hostility is rare; sometimes there is bewildering veneration. When touring India with England in the mid-1980s it was a surprise to witness how much interest, which occasionally stretched towards adoration, was generated. There would be large crowds outside the hotels when we returned there after play especially on the chaotic Chowringhee Road in Calcutta – though there was far more excitement whenever a bus containing the Indian side turned up. For a while I was rather boosted by the fact that when I emerged from the bus I would be surrounded by fans seeking an autograph – until I heard them shouting quizzically, 'Pocock, Pocock? Edmonds? Where's Iron Bottom?' (He was in England having a tour off, as it happens.)

In the wake of India's World Cup victory in 1983 every seat would be sold for the ODIs on that tour, and at the old ground in Nagpur one ramshackle wooden stand collapsed while play was going on. It was a nasty moment but it was deemed to be such a routine occurrence that we just played on. The crowds in India were noisy, and they relished a home victory, but they were never hostile – and, as we came to realize in Nagpur, they were not always safe.

Nor were they really hostile at Taunton, but they were undoubtedly partisan. We never tired of their chants. 'We're all part of Rosey's army... And we'll really shake 'em up when we win the Gillette Cup 'cos Somerset are the greatest cricket team...' Such chants were a relatively new phenomenon at our county grounds and had one or two older members spluttering into their beer, but the young players out in the middle welcomed them.

For one-day matches there was seldom a spare seat at Taunton in the late 1970s; many spectators were content to stand all day. There was little space at the tiny ground and even less security. Years later, a highly respectable old supporter explained to me how the crowd swelled so mysteriously for those one-day games. 'We always had an empty matchbox with us and once we had entered the ground down by the old Stragglers pavilion [where the groundsman now keeps his equipment] we would put our tickets into the box and toss it over the wall to our mates. This process would be repeated many times.'

Sometimes opposition clubs lost out on vital revenue as well. In 1976 the Somerset fans travelled in their thousands to Cardiff for the final John Player League game of the season. Victory would see Somerset become the champions – but we lost by one run, of course. That morning, the Somerset fans had turned up so early that there were no gatemen on duty at Sophia Gardens, so they all wandered into the ground and took their place in the stands or on the grass. Before long, the forlorn Glamorgan secretary – Wilf Wooller, no less – was looking on with horror. He sent his staff into the stands carrying buckets, into which he hoped the appropriate gate money would be thrown by the Somerset supporters. Apparently this exercise was nowhere near as successful as he had hoped.

If not hostile, Taunton could be an intimidating venue for the opposition, though it helped if Joel Garner and Ian Botham had been named in the Somerset side. That was certainly the case when Kent were the visitors in 1979 in the quarter-final of the knockout competition. Joel and Ian and a capacity crowd at full volume really did shake 'em up in the Gillette Cup. Somerset defended an inadequate 190 with Garner and Botham on song. The crowd caught the mood brilliantly and roared. I was twelfth man for that game and the only place to sit was by the old pavilion gate. From there, I watched every Kent batsman come and go and I could see how their faces grew paler and paler as every wicket fell. They were bowled out for 60.

Around this time our captain, Brian Rose, considered putting a sign up high on the wall that would be visible just before leaving the old pavilion, saying 'This is Taunton' and copying what we had all heard about at Liverpool FC: 'This is Anfield'. Taunton became a fortress because of the home crowd, which was so close to the action and so raucous in their support of their boys. That still applies, I'm pleased to say, although the stands are far more palatial now. One reason for this may be that there are fewer distractions down in the

West Country; there is also a sense of identity that results in the supporters being so eager to get behind the locals. And it helps that the county ground at Taunton is a delightful place to watch cricket or, indeed, to escape the cricket if it is dreary – the High Street is only a hundred yards away. By and large, abroad and at home, the out-of-town stadia do not work well while the more intimate grounds near the centre of town do.

The Somerset fans did their best to take over Lord's when we played in finals there. They came with their banners and their smocks and their cider and their determination to drown out the supporters of our opponents. They largely succeeded, which cheered us up in the dressing room. Then the final wicket would be taken or the final runs struck and the sacred Lord's turf would be invaded as the players sprinted from the middle to the haven of the dressing room. Not that anyone was going to hurt us, but within seconds it was impossible to move on that outfield. This was standard procedure on our cricket grounds in the 1980s.

I've just glimpsed an old photo of Ian Botham leaving the field after his epic century at Headingley against Australia in 1981. The outfield is packed with enthralled spectators. The fans just wanted to see him at close quarters and, maybe, to touch him. Their eyes look on in wonder. And there is no sign of any stewards in their yellow bibs eager to demonstrate their rugby-tackling prowess. I'm just trying to picture Ben Stokes leaving the field in 2019 after an innings that was even more astonishing; he is embracing Jack Leach but the spectators are still in the stands; they may have been looking on in wonder as well – while watching the big screen.

We were wary of those invasions but they were considered an occupational hazard. At the end of England's World Cup semi-final at Old Trafford in 1983, when the game was up with India needing one more run with six wickets and five overs to spare, just about all the England fielders had drifted to the off side near the pavilion to ensure the swiftest exit back to the dressing room.

It was more entertaining – and more chaotic – towards the end of the World Cup final at Lord's in 1975, when Australia's last pair, Dennis Lillee and Jeff Thomson, were together. They needed 26 runs off two overs, a seemingly impossible task then since all the fielders could be stationed on the boundary. First the crowd invaded when they thought that Thomson was run out, but umpire Dickie Bird's finger stayed down. Eventually order was restored. Then Thomson scooped a catch to Roy Fredericks but neither the crowd nor Jim Laker – 'That's it. That's it,' he concluded on the TV – registered that a no-ball had just been bowled. Meanwhile Fredericks shied at the stumps and missed them, whereupon the ball disappeared among the onrushing hordes. The batsmen kept running. Bird had his hat and various sweaters snatched as he attempted to wave them all away; the other umpire, Tom Spencer, just looked on in horror. When the field was eventually cleared, Thomson asked Spencer, 'How many are you giving us for that?' The response of 'Two' did not impress. 'Pig's arse, we've been running up and down all afternoon.' At the other end Bird asked Lillee, 'How many have you run?' 'You should be counting,' replied Lillee, 'but I make it about seventeen.' Soon after, Thomson was properly run out and the West Indies, it was decided, had won the inaugural final by 17 runs. This was an experiment that just had to be repeated, preferably without so many pitch invasions.

Hopefully we have learned not to take all these fans for granted now. The cricket in 2020 was a brave and remarkably successful attempt to keep the game alive despite the absence of any spectators. Television may be the cash cow of cricket, but without the fans in the stands this precious product is hugely diminished. The players, the county treasurers and even the TV executives should never again take for granted the live cricket fan, who has taken the trouble to turn up.

By the same token, nor will spectators take the game for granted after being forced into exile in 2020. Hopefully they will all flock back in 2021, not just to the high-profile international matches but also to the county game. I have seen at Taunton – and this applies at Worcester, Hove or Chelmsford, I'm sure – how a certain space in a certain stand becomes the social hub (though they might not call it that) of groups of senior supporters who go to their local county ground not only because they enjoy the cricket but also because they value the camaraderie of like-minded people with whom they can engage and perhaps become friends while the match goes on in the distance. Improve the Wi-Fi at our grounds – in an era when working from home becomes ever more popular – and some employees might even make the Marcus Trescothick Stand their 'home office' for the day.

7

Failure

'You're messing with my career, Darrell.'

Mark Ramprakash, Lord's, 1998

R. C. ROBERTSON-GLASGOW, cricket writer nonpareil, once famously asked, 'Who ever hoped like a cricketer?' A gloomy corollary comes to mind: 'Who ever failed like a cricketer?' We fail all the time, even the good ones. There is the evidence in black and white for all to see on the scorecard: J. Root b Cummins 0 (Old Trafford, 2019); B. Stokes b Boult 0 (Auckland, 2018).

It happens to the very best – even to Don Bradman. As E. J. Thribb would have it in *Private Eye*, 'Bowled Hollies 0. So farewell then, Sir Don.' Mind you, Bradman endured the agonies of failure less frequently than any batsman in the history of the game. Apparently he was once asked by an aspiring youngster how best to come out of a rough trot with the bat and he replied, 'Sorry, son. Can't help you there. It never really happened to me.' As ever, the pragmatist rather than the charmer.

I decided to check this out. In Bradman's fifty-two Tests he never went more than five innings without scoring a half-century. This little glimpse of failure took place at the start of the 1934 tour of England, whereupon he compensated in the final two Tests with innings of 304 and 244. Point proven? I thought so. Then I checked out Joe Root. After 100 Test appearances, he had never gone more than seven innings without a half-century. For Steve Smith, I discovered, the longest barren trot is the same as Bradman's – only five consecutive innings under 50 after seventy-seven matches. By this measure, the difference between Bradman and the rest is not as stark as anticipated. With apologies to all the whiz-kids at CricViz, we may have to stick to the old measure of batting averages.

Anyway, the thesis stands. Great batsmen fail; moderate batsmen fail quite a lot; poor batsmen fail very frequently yet they still come back for more. It is no wonder the game is such a source of torment. A cheap dismissal is like a little death (though not in the French sense). All is well with the world: you are in charge, dismissing the ball from your presence, dictating the course of the match. Then one mistake, one brilliant delivery or one moment of ill fortune, and it's all over – barring a successful review in an international match. Thus we lurch from contentment to despair in the blink of an eye.

I'm not sure any sport creates such distress so frequently. We might remember Doug Sanders missing that short putt at St Andrews in 1970, Devon Loch collapsing just short of the finishing line in the 1956 Grand National, Don Fox missing the kick in front of the posts in the 1968 Rugby League Cup final, the famous penalty shoot-out misses of Stuart Pearce,

Chris Waddle and Gareth Southgate, or Greg Norman's disintegration against Nick Faldo at Augusta in 1996. But these are unusual, even freakish events. Every cricketer has to be prepared to cope with the pain of sudden failure on just about every day of his professional life. No wonder dressing rooms suddenly become noisier, more relaxed places when the rain starts pouring down. It means the chances of failing on that particular day are fast receding.

No one fails so obviously or so publicly as a batsman dismissed within moments of arriving at the crease, which helps to explain why cricket is such an excruciating game to play and a mesmerizing one to watch. There was, for example, a delicious pleasure in watching David Gower bat but this was heightened by the knowledge that he might get out at any moment. It is worse for a batsman because the failure is so final. After a nightmare over, a bowler has the chance to atone in the next one (provided he can persuade his captain to keep him on) but the batsman just has to go, often in a state of fury, despair and anguish. 'You're messing with my career, Darrell,' said Mark Ramprakash to umpire Hair when he was erroneously given out caught behind against South Africa in the Lord's Test of 1998, an observation that cost him an £850 fine and a suspended one-match ban.

In my experience the great players often cope with bleak failure by deciding it wasn't really their fault. In my early days I'd revel in the explanations of Ian Botham ('Should have tried to hit it harder and I would have cleared him'), Viv Richards ('missing leg, man') and Brian Close ('wrong-flavoured chewing gum delivered by twelfth man'). The great players cannot allow their self-belief to be dented by any suggestion of their own frailty. Which makes sense. If they did, they wouldn't be so great. Of course, that impression of infallibility can be just that: an impression. Just once I remember Botham going out to bat after saying, 'There's no way I'll get a run here.' That was on a dank day at Old Trafford in May 1981 soon after his tour of the Caribbean as captain of England. Michael Holding was bowling fast for Lancashire against Somerset and Ian had not yet exorcized his memories of that tour. He was indeed out for a duck, dismissed by Holding, and his mortality was confirmed (mind you, he then bowled Somerset to victory along with Joel Garner). The same happened with Sunil Gavaskar for less obvious reasons when he was playing for Somerset in 1980. 'Don't open with me today,' he said as we prepared for our second innings at Trent Bridge. 'But you're our star opening batsman.' Out he went and he returned moments later for a duck. He was trying but his premonition had been correct. Even the great players have their frailties; it is just that they do not reveal them so often.

Once I earwigged a mid-pitch conversation between the Warwickshire openers of the 1980s, Dennis Amiss – by then a veteran and one of England's most prolific and dependable batsmen – and K. D. Smith, a relative novice. To my surprise, it was Amiss who was anxiously seeking reassurance: 'Is my bat coming down straight, K. D.? Are my feet moving properly?' How could Amiss be the one riddled with self-doubt? Maybe it was simply the fact that Amiss had played so long that he had come to realize nothing can be guaranteed in this game. At the start of one season, my Somerset colleague Peter Roebuck, an established county batsman at the time, queried how he was ever going to score another run. I tried to reassure him by saying he would score 1200 in the season at an average close to 40 – as usual. This did not seem to help him much at the time. But, come September, that is what he had delivered. It is so much easier looking on from the outside. During the break caused by Covid-19 in 2020 I even heard Jason Roy, a batsman who has never seemed short of confidence, wondering aloud whether he would be able to bat after such a long absence from the game. As it happened, he did struggle when play resumed.

There are a variety of reactions to failure. Ramprakash – such a measured, calculating batsman in his pomp – was noted for his unfettered fury upon dismissal, not just when he had been on the receiving end of a bad decision, a trait that led to a nickname of 'Bloodaxe'. He once demolished a helmet back in the dressing room after being run out when playing for Surrey; sadly it was not his but the one belonging to his captain, Adam Hollioake, who had to have a word – after a suitable cooling-off period. There are certain players who prompt a swift exodus of teammates from the dressing room when dismissed, and Ramprakash may have been one of them.

Ben Stokes, out first ball in the Caribbean in 2014, broke a bone in his wrist when smashing a dressing-room locker as he sought to let off steam after another failure. Matthew Hayden – to the ultimate delight of his colleagues – once kicked a wicker chair at Sydney, whereupon his foot became wedged and he began hopping around the dressing room in a forlorn attempt to remove this new, unwanted appendage. Like many others, Geoffrey Boycott sometimes wrapped a towel over his head as he tried to come to terms with a recent disaster. It is well documented that he held this pose for a very long time in Wellington, New Zealand in 1978 after Ian Botham had fulfilled his promise to run him out so that England had more time to bowl out the Kiwis in the final innings of the match.

The West Indies batsman Carlisle Best (Tino's great-uncle), who played eight Tests between 1986 and 1990, sometimes performed an unusual ritual after dismissal. At the crease Best would often give a running commentary of his innings: 'A glorious pull shot races away to the boundary. You can't bowl there to Carlisle Best.' Even more entertaining, according to Ottis Gibson, his Bajan colleague, was the sight and sound of Best after being dismissed, sitting in the dressing room opposite his bat, which he had propped up on a nearby chair. Best would enter into an agonized conversation with this blameless chunk of wood: 'Why did you do that? It was a terrible shot you played... What were you doing out there?'

At the other end of the scale was my old friend, Chris Tavaré. When he returned to the dressing room after dismissal, it was impossible to tell whether he had scored 0 or 100. He would not say a word before carefully returning his bat to its place in the neatest cricket coffin on the circuit. Tavaré, I suggest, was in the minority. As for me, I was more of a sulker than a ranter, which was of no benefit to anyone.

The problem for cricketers, especially batsmen, is that so much time is available for dire deliberation. Imagine being an opener in a Test match and being dismissed in the first over. It may well be another three days before you have the chance to atone. During that period the mind can cause havoc; there is so much time to brood over the latest failure: the job is to score runs and I have not scored any, which is plain for all to see, so I must be bad at my job, worthless, contributing nothing. From there it is not such a great leap from considering myself to be a bad batsman to thinking I'm a bad person, in which case a dangerous downward spiral is under way.

The anguish is amplified in Test cricket, when the whole world seems to be watching and the experts are analysing your frailties in minute detail. Do I stare endlessly at my laptop at a replay of the dismissal and gloomily conclude that Nasser Hussain and Mike Atherton are right in the commentary box as they deconstruct all my flaws: the head is in the wrong place, the left leg is too braced and in any case the front/ back foot should be somewhere else? So there are already at least three things to clog up the mind when I next take guard in front of the cameras. Or should I just adopt the Botham approach, which rarely led to the conclusion 'mea culpa, skip'?

The torment can hit anyone, not just the novice. In November 2013 Jonathan Trott was playing his forty-ninth Test match for England, at the Gabba in Brisbane, and it was a terrifying spectacle. In his second innings against Australia's quickest bowler, Mitchell Johnson, it became apparent that Trott – a stalwart in the England side for the previous four years – had no idea what he was doing; he was out of control; his body would not connect to any instructions from his brain. So he batted way out of character, recklessly, in a nightmarish daze and he soon fell victim to Johnson. It transpired that Trott was mentally unfit to play in that match; he was prob- ably unfit to embark on that tour to Australia but wishful thinking and his superb record had dictated his presence there. He left the tour after this Test, which was the only feasible decision available. Eighteen months later he tried to return as an England cricketer in the Caribbean, where he played three more Test matches but it did not work. After his experience in Brisbane, it was brave even to try.

Maybe it is slightly easier for bowlers, although there is no hiding place for them – a failing batsman can at least disappear swiftly to the anonymity of the dressing room. Andy Bull of the *Guardian* interviewed Scott Boswell ten years after his career-ending appearance in a Lord's final for Leicestershire against Somerset in 2003. It was the first time Boswell had spoken publicly about his woe. In the NatWest semi-final he had delivered career-best figures of 4-44 against Lancashire, but his second over at Lord's – on what should have been the greatest day of his cricketing life – felt as if it would never end. Boswell had been uneasy about his form ahead of the match and he told Andy about his second over in the game when Somerset's Marcus Trescothick was on strike:

'He looked as though he was 50 yards away. He was like a tiny dot. I just couldn't see him. Then I bowled a wide and I heard the noise of the crowd. I bowled a second wide, and the noise got louder and louder and louder.' His muscles grew tight. His fingers grew tense. He began to sweat. 'I just couldn't let go of the ball. I wanted to get on with it, so I began to rush. The more I panicked, the more I rushed.' He lost his run-up. The pitch, already on a slope, seemed to tilt sharper beneath his feet. He makes it sound like vertigo. [...] 'Jesus Christ, I am going to be bowling here all bloody day. [...] I was thinking: "I just want to get this over, I just want to get this over" but it kept going and going and going, wide after wide after wide.' Some flew to slip, others towards fine leg.

The footage is harrowing. In all there would be fourteen deliveries in that over. Unsurprisingly, Boswell did not bowl again in the match. Afterwards most of his colleagues – the exception being Jimmy Ormond – declined to talk to him about his experience; it was too uncomfortable. In fact, there was just one more over for Leicestershire later in the season in the John Player League, which went for 18 runs, whereupon Boswell feigned cramp and ran off the field. At the age of 26 his contract was not renewed. He may not have had the purest of actions but it had served him well enough throughout 2003; it was the occasion that paralysed him at the end of his run-up at Lord's. This was the cruellest moment. Cricket may be a team game but it is one in which individuals can be ruthlessly exposed; there is no hiding place.

It may be that the Lancashire left-arm spinner, Simon Kerrigan, experienced something similar on his Test debut, at The Oval against Australia in 2013. A pinnacle in anyone's career turned out to be an ugly ordeal for Kerrigan, one of two debutants on the day. (The other was Chris Woakes, who began nervily yet survived and then prospered as an England cricketer.) It was tough to watch, but nowhere near as tough as experiencing the torment out in the middle with the ball stuck in your hand. For Kerrigan, The Oval, with a capacity crowd looking on, suddenly became the loneliest place in the world.

That evening I tried to explain to *Guardian* readers what Kerrigan might have been going through. 'The problem is that your fingers feel like pork sausages, sweaty pork sausages at that. Meanwhile the ball somehow acquires the qualities of a melon; it will not fit in your hand. The batsman has a bat the size of a barn door and you only have seven fielders out there to defend the incredibly short boundaries.' Kerrigan went for 28 runs in two overs mostly against Shane Watson, who could not believe his luck, and then captain Alastair Cook felt compelled to take him off. After twelve deliveries Kerrigan was in crisis mode, desperate for another over but also terrified of what might happen if he was given another go. It soon became apparent that he had no idea where the ball was going to land, which was never the case when he was playing for Lancashire. A slightly quirky action with the arm over the perpendicular was no longer an asset, but it was the occasion that undermined him – and scarred him for years to come. He returned to Lancashire but never came close to playing for England again; his home county released him in 2018 and he signed for Northamptonshire in 2020.

Kerrigan was not the first left-arm spinner to experience a form of the dreaded yips. Fred Swarbrook was a successful spinner for Derbyshire in the 1970s, yet by 1978 he could bowl beautifully in the nets but had no idea where the ball would land in the middle, a mystery that he never really resolved. One year Norman Gifford, the most dependable of pros, realized he did not have a clue which foot to put forward when starting his run-up. Phil Edmonds had his moments of panic too. On the tour of India in 1984/85 he completely lost his run-up. As a consequence he bowled after taking just one tentative step. 'I suppose the reason was an over-anxiety to succeed,' he wrote afterwards. He recognized that other left-armers had had a similar experience 'but I could not believe it was happening to me.' Fortunately Edmonds was so strong and blessed with such a pure action that the inability to take his usual five paces up to the crease did not inconvenience him much. If anything, the affliction may have diminished his flights of fancy, which meant he became a more miserly bowler. Keith Medlycott of Surrey was another gifted spinner who was forced to retire at 26 soon after he had been picked for England's tour of the Caribbean in 1990.

The provenance of the yips remains a mystery but it seems as if they are more likely to attack left-armers. Off-spinners are very capable of bowling badly but are far less likely to lose all control, so they are generally spared the nightmare of not knowing whether the over is ever going to end.

There is another source of anguish for the failing cricketer: dropping catches. This painful experience comes in two categories. The first is the humiliating fluffing of the simplest of chances, the ones your great-grandad could catch in his sleep. Goalkeepers will understand this peculiar torment better than most. It is a lonely, incomprehensible aberration. Two examples spring to mind: Mike Gatting at silly point dropping Kiran More in Madras off Ian Salisbury in 1993, and Joe Denly at short mid-wicket spilling Kane Williamson off Jofra Archer in 2019.

The second category contains the missed chances that are remembered because of their dire consequences. Graham Gooch was dropped behind the stumps by the aforementioned More on 36 at Lord's in 1990 and he went on to score 333. Durham's wicketkeeper Chris Scott dropped Brian Lara on 18 when he was playing for Warwickshire at Edgbaston in 1994. Scott is supposed to have morosely mumbled to his slip cordon, 'I bet he goes on to make a hundred now.' In fact, Lara finished with 501 not out. South Africa's Herschelle Gibbs, celebrating prematurely, dropped Steve Waugh and – according to legend – the World Cup in a vital match at Headingley in 1999. Maybe England would not have regained the Ashes in 2005 if Shane Warne had caught Kevin Pietersen at slip at The Oval on the final day of the series. Meanwhile, Nathan Lyon's failure to gather the ball to run out Jack Leach at Headingley in 2019 still lingers in the memory on both sides of the globe.

The list could go on and on and on, just like the agony of the errant fielder, who only wants to disappear down the nearest hole. (Here speaks a man who dropped three catches off Ian Botham within the space of fifteen minutes at Bournemouth in 1976, when stationed – mistakenly with hindsight – in the slip cordon.) 'Look forward to the next one,' they shout. Like hell you do.

So now you may understand why I wrote in 1989, upon being invited to be the *Observer*'s cricket correspondent, that I regarded playing the game as more difficult than writing about it. What do I think after over three decades in the press box since then? Exactly the same. We notice every error out on the field, small or large, from our comfortable perch and we routinely jot down the details – 'What was the score when he was dropped? And how many did he have? How many have they scored since then?' – and then we relay the gory details to our readers. Few fail so publicly or so obviously as a professional cricketer. That's why they deserve admiration and sympathy. By contrast, an incorrect fact from the sages of the press box, a ridiculous assertion or the odd split infinitive – if any of these blemishes escape the notice of the sub-editors – warrant little or no attention.

8

Food

'George Gunn lunches at 1.30 p.m.'

George Gunn

MAN MAY NOT be able to live by bread alone but we all know how some fresh sandwiches at teatime can cheer us all up. Food is at the forefront of a cricketer's mind far more frequently than is the case among other sportspeople. A cricket match can take so long that it has to be interrupted by some form of sustenance, and an anxious mind in need of comfort and escape from the torment of trying to master such a damn difficult game is easily tempted to spend a lot of time contemplating those meals – as well as eating them. This became apparent right from the start of my professional career.

In 1974 the food at Taunton was much more of an issue than a wide-eyed teenager had ever anticipated. The players took their lunch in the old indoor school; it was prepared in a rudimentary kitchen nearby, out of which came the most basic fare and it did not meet with the universal approval of those about to eat it. Merv Kitchen – the stoutest of Somerset men, who would become a much respected umpire at both county and Test level – was a senior man on the staff, an unofficial shop steward and a formidable trencherman. The staple diet for lunch on match days was some sweaty ham, with tired (or, on a bad day, utterly exhausted) lettuce and boiled potatoes that somehow ended up being both hard and cold, all of which would be served up by the venerable Ethel, who was not so far removed from the Julie Walters character in Victoria Wood's 'Two Soups' sketch. Everything would then be desperately smothered in salad cream (if there was any left in the bottle). Merv, in particular, would be unimpressed by this fare and this prompted a familiar monologue: 'This food is disgusting and it's the same every day. How are we supposed to run around the field all afternoon on this diet? It's never right. Oh and push the spuds this way, will you? And do you want that last bit of ham? Pass it over, then.'

Merv had a point. Indeed, there were occasions when the twelfth man – who might be me or Peter Roebuck or Phil Slocombe – was prevailed upon to take orders in the morning before the first team headed out into the field and then to go to the fish and chip shop outside the ground before delivering lunch to those players who had decided they could no longer stomach any more of the offerings eventually served up by Ethel.

The food improved in 1981. This was when the new pavilion on the other side of the ground alongside the River Tone was completed (there have been several others built since then). On the first floor were the dressing rooms for the players and the umpires (for some reason, the home dressing room housed a full-sized snooker table for several seasons), the committee room and the secretary's office. On the ground floor were palatial dining facilities for players and public, some proper kitchens, a proper chef and a welcome absence of sweaty ham.

Maybe the food was too good now. The nutritionists had yet to make their interventions, so when we all rolled up for a Sunday League match at around 12.30 p.m. for a 2 p.m. start, the first port of call was the dining room. What did we eat? Well, it was Sunday so it would usually be roast beef, Yorkshire pudding, roast potatoes, lashings of gravy and some apple pie to finish. And custard, of course. Lovely. Within the hour we would be out on the field in the harum-scarum of a 40-over match yet no one thought to quibble about the components of our pre-match lunch.

Those trips to the fish and chip shop by the twelfth man were no longer necessary. Suddenly Somerset had some of the best food around, though the indomitable Nancy Doyle, who ruled the players' kitchens at Lord's for thirty-five years, was still the most beloved – and possibly the most feared – cook on the county circuit. Nancy would produce feasts vast enough to satisfy the young Mike Gatting. The Middlesex captain Mike Brearley once asked her to limit the quantity of food available to his players at lunchtime since he thought it might be hampering their performances throughout the afternoon – a request she shunned, which immediately increased her popularity among just about everyone on the county circuit. Mike Selvey, Middlesex's opening bowler at the time, has recalled the day Brearley met his match:

The fiercest bouncer received by Brearley was not from any of the whizzbangs, who prowled cricket three or four decades ago. Instead it was sent down with blistering verbal venom by someone who was five feet high when on tiptoe, fiery, female and very Irish. Brearley had approached Nancy again to suggest that a soup starter, roast lamb with roast potatoes, chips and vegetables, a dessert with a choice of custard, cream or ice cream and cheeseboard was not ideal refuelling for an afternoon of professional sport. 'Tell you what, Michael,' she spat, drawing herself up and stabbing her forefinger into his chest like a woodpecker at a tree, 'I won't tell you how to fecking bat if you don't tell me how to fecking cook. OK?'

Like the Roman general confronted by the threat of Hannibal, Fabius Cunctator, Brearley knew when it was prudent to withdraw quietly.

The climate had changed by 2013 and so had the menu, especially if you were playing for England. As the national team was starting their tour in Australia, a document outlining the team's dietary requirements was leaked to a delighted Aussie press corps. The team's coach, Andy Flower (a man who leaves very little to chance), and his performance nutritionist, Chris Rosimus, had compiled eighty-two pages of guidance for those preparing the food for his squad at the Australian Test grounds. It was not designed for public consumption but that was where it ended up as the Australian sports desks gleefully seized upon this wonderful windfall. England now looked a ludicrously precious outfit. The list was never-ending but to give you a flavour: at the ground, pumpkin seed and goji berry breakfast bars had to be available to the England players and staff before the game; quinoa, cranberry and feta salad would be one option at lunchtime; after the game, Moroccan-spiced griddled chicken fillets with lime and coriander mayo should be on offer, along with lamb and pea kofta kebabs with mint yoghurt and piripiri breaded tofu with tomato salsa. What would Merv have made of all that? It's hard to be sure; he did not like many frills, so perhaps he would still have opted for Ethel's sweaty ham.

Professional cricketers are, of course, pampered now, as are the press at the majority of international venues in the United Kingdom and overseas. The best curries that I have devoured have come out of massive vats at the back of press boxes in India. At home, Lord's maintains its reputation for wonderful food (and plenty of it), with Edgbaston providing the sternest competition since the redevelopments there.

It is possible for the weak-willed media person to put on almost half a stone at either venue throughout the course of a five-day Test match – you may surmise, all too briefly, how I know that. Indeed, one of the best arguments for switching to four-day Test cricket is that this might help in the struggle against increasing obesity among the press corps. For several years, at the back of the press box there would also be a sweet counter, courtesy of the ECB's sponsors, and I discovered it was practically impossible to complete a match report without the assistance of half a dozen Cadbury Eclairs and the odd Curly Wurly. Sadly – I mean *sensibly* – such temptations have been removed, as have the glasses of wine that were offered by Cornhill every lunchtime when I started in the press box in 1990. That link between the purveyors of junk food and cricket was renewed, however, when the sponsors for The Hundred teams were revealed: a range of KP snacks products. Despite the ridicule in the press, this union made some sense: junk food for junk cricket.

Cricketers – and cricket writers – tend to adhere to Napoleon's mantra: they like to march on their stomachs. They have always done so, as the tale of George Gunn – a Nottinghamshire batsman for three decades either side of the First World War – demonstrates. In his day, play usually began at 11.30 a.m. with the players withdrawing for lunch at 1.30 p.m., but occasionally there might be a change to the schedule with the game starting at 12 noon and lunch being taken at 2 p.m. The story goes that in one of these games Gunn, having taken umbrage that play was still going on, got out deliberately half an hour before the interval; he tucked his bat under his arm and headed towards the pavilion, announcing that 'George Gunn lunches at 1.30.' Upon his arrival in the dining room he would not have been greeted by piripiri breaded tofu.

So much for lunch. Tea was always a bit of a scramble for a county side in the field. It was never the leisurely experience that we associate with the village green: strawberries and cream as well as an assortment of bake-off treasures, which the umpires would never dream of deserting until everyone was satisfied. In the professional dressing room, priorities were different especially for the smoker. In the space of a quarter of an hour, it was necessary to consume a cup of tea, a few sandwiches and two cigarettes before the resumption of play. There was not much time for conversation, tactical or otherwise. It was a more leisurely undertaking if your side was batting, although here some regulation was necessary. Too often the two batsmen who had been valiantly fending off the opposition's fiercest bowlers out in the middle would return to the dressing room to find the sandwich tray empty.

The team dinner was a less rushed affair but it only took place before special occasions. In the 1980s any newcomer to the England side would be required to sit alongside the chairman of selectors on the eve of a Test match. So before my Test debut, at Headingley in 1982, I sat next to P. B. H. May and the sadness is that I cannot remember anything of our conversation. What an opportunity missed – on my part. Towards the end of the meal there would be some words from the chairman and the captain, all rather stilted as we were on our best behaviour, and at the end Ian Botham would insist on going to the bar for a pint or two – to ensure that we were properly relaxed before the trials ahead.

Team dinners at Somerset were infrequent but more boisterous; they only happened on the eve of Lord's finals and they tended to be noisy affairs. There was a determination among the players to enjoy the club's rare hospitality to the full. The port might be passed, not necessarily in the right direction, and at some point we might attempt some sort of tactical talk ahead of our big match. For about the only time in the season, we would try to analyse our opponents. Once again Botham would be to the fore. 'Don't worry about him. I'll take care of him,' he might say. Or he would insist that so-and-so should on no account be bounced, advice he contradicted right from the very start of his spell the following day. Oh so shrewdly, one or two of us might point out how key opposition batsmen 'might struggle against Joel'. Then the arguments would begin: 'He's a strong leg-side player,' someone would interject with absolute certainty. 'No, he's not: he loves to carve through the covers.' 'He likes to cut.' 'No, he likes to drive.' It would get increasingly animated, occasionally ill-tempered, and then captain Brian Rose would spread his arms in exasperation and try to terminate proceedings by saying it was time for bed.

It wasn't very scientific, but somehow over the years it became a relaxing ritual. In fact, before the 1979 Gillette Cup final (which would see Somerset winning a trophy for the first time in their history), captain Brian Rose decided to accept an invitation for the entire team to go to dinner with Weston-super-Mare-born John Cleese on the eve of the match. This proved to be a very good idea since it was such an unusual and enjoyable distraction to the trials ahead.

Sometimes a less relaxing ritual is the after-dinner speech that many cricketers find themselves giving. Often the meal can be as taxing as the speech itself. In the little Devon village of Shobrooke up in the hills beyond Crediton, they still recall Viv Richards attending their annual cricket dinner back in the 1980s. It is hard to fathom how Viv ended up there. It must have taken place during his benefit year since he would hardly have committed himself to such an event otherwise. Viv was always meticulously polite with supporters, but he never really relished mingling with them for long – unlike Joel Garner, who was a pied piper at Taunton with queues forever forming behind him as he wandered around the ground while we were batting. Viv was not so at ease in public and he preferred to keep his distance. He could be shy in the company of strangers and he was not especially adept at small talk. Yet here he was, inside the quaint thatched pavilion at Shobrooke, and, as the guest of honour, he was naturally seated at the top table.

Next to Viv was the octogenarian president of the club, another shy man. He was not a particularly ardent cricket fan but he was the president because he was the local farmer who owned the field upon which Shobrooke's cricketers gratefully played. All round the pavilion there was the buzz of cheerful conversation as the dinner began – except on the top table. Viv was sitting there without uttering a word and the old farmer did not seem to have anything to say either. So there was a conversational vacuum, which gradually became more and more uncomfortable. Eventually the old president gave way to the urgency to break the silence and he turned to Viv with a question. In a dialect fashioned in mid-Devon for eight decades, he asked, 'Do you play much of this cricket, then?' Viv's response has not been recorded but we can surmise that this proved rather a long evening for the greatest batsman of the era.

9

Twelfth Man

'I think they must be mad.'

Phil Edmonds, 1985

WE ALL GET dropped somewhere along the way – even Don Bradman was dropped once – and the sense of rejection lingers. It is worse when you consider yourself to be a linchpin of the side, only to discover the captain is ambling in your direction to explain that you are the man who will be 'carrying the drinks', which is not a very cheery euphemism. Carrying the drinks – along with all the other duties of a twelfth man, who is part batman, part emergency fielder, part skivvy and part amateur psychologist – is not much fun.

Being dropped does not always bring out the best in a professional sportsman (Geoffrey Boycott was left out of the England team in 1967 for 'selfish batting' after compiling 246 against India, and I gather he may have become a bit grumpy as a consequence) but for most of us it is an occupational hazard. In Test cricket neither Alastair Cook nor Marcus Trescothick were ever dropped (although the latter was forced to withdraw his availability), but they are the exceptions. In the twenty-first century this process often comes with a lot of flannel because being dropped in an inclusive world can be seen as such a cataclysmic event. 'No, no! He's not dropped; he's just being rested or rotated,' we are told. Don't be misled. Modern captains and coaches may not enjoy the ructions of leaving someone out, but they generally like to have their strongest team out there, though in the winter of 2020/21 England decided that they had to juggle the personnel in their team because of a new phenomenon: the danger of 'bubble fatigue'.

The dropping I remember most clearly was at Taunton in July of 1981, mainly because I was the one being left out. By then I was a capped player in the Somerset side and a regular in the team – or so I thought. We were playing Sussex in the Championship and, on the morning of the match, captain Brian Rose told me I wasn't playing. I had not expected that. I was mildly stunned; this was not the moment for a long discussion about such an (obviously flawed) decision since Rose had to go and toss up. He was a busy man, but for me there was suddenly ample time to contemplate how the day was going to pan out rather differently than expected. Instead of bowling to John Barclay and Paul Parker, a contrasting challenge, or facing Garth le Roux and Geoff Arnold, I would indeed be ferrying drinks, lunches and sweaters. That had not been part of the plan on my drive to the ground.

Upon hearing the bad news, there came a confusion of thoughts: obviously I wanted Somerset to win the match, but it would have been preferable for them to do so while it became crystal clear to the captain – and everyone else – that he had picked the wrong team. There could be no rejoicing at any teammates' failures (at least, not in public) as I mooched around the balcony, even though there was plenty of opportunity to do that in the game against Sussex. Soon Somerset were 23-3, and inside 25 overs they were bowled out for 104. There could be no whistling as I delivered the dismissed batsmen their statutory glass of orange squash on their return to the dressing room, although most of them did not have much of a thirst to quench; only three of them had managed to reach double figures. I tried to be earnestly sympathetic. 'Bad toss to lose. Dodgy wicket. Fine delivery. Arnold's a great bowler when he's on song, isn't he? More squash?'

They let me play in the Sunday League match that interrupted this game after the first day. I took 2-23 from my eight overs and then remained unbeaten at the crease on 14 not out when we won by four wickets. Job done, before I returned to my mundane twelfth-man duties. Back in the three-day match, Somerset rallied after their first-innings collapse but they lost the game by six wickets, one of only two defeats in the Championship that summer. I was as grim-faced as everyone else at the end. I made sure that was the case. And I was back in the side for the next match. There is one silver lining to being dropped and the team subsequently losing: without scoring a run or taking a wicket, your reputation is enhanced.

In my dotage and long after retirement from the game, I often find myself advocating that we should be less fearful of dropping players, though I probably did not feel that way back in 1981. Look at the careers of Andrew Strauss, Ian Bell and even Joe Root. All of them were dropped from the England team when established Test cricketers; all of them were stunned and hurt but then rapidly recognized what they were missing and took steps to refresh and improve. And to ensure it never happened again. The good ones always come back. At various points Australia dropped Ricky Ponting, Shane Warne and Glenn McGrath.

At international level there was never the same sense of surprise when I was made twelfth man. I was never a regular in the Test team. I did play four Tests in a row on England's 1983/84 winter tour; and it might have been five. I was in contention for the Christchurch Test in New Zealand at the start of February 1984, another game that did not go according to plan after my omission. The skies were dark, there had been a lot of rain in the South Island, and the pitch at Lancaster Park – a forbidding rugby stadium in the winter – was damp. England had an injury crisis among their pace bowlers, which resulted in the emergency call-up of Tony Pigott, the Sussex paceman, who was wintering in New Zealand. He postponed his wedding to be in Christchurch.

The pre-match routine for the England squad never changed in that era. We formed a large circle seventy-five minutes before the start of play and then we would perform our loosening exercises under the direction of the physio, Bernard Thomas, who stood in the middle giving instructions. We did the same exercises in the same order on every day of the tour. As we did them on the morning of the Test on the practice ground behind the stands, I was well aware that our final eleven had yet to be announced. I sensed that, if a spinner were to be selected, I would play ahead of the left-armer, Nick Cook, who had struggled to make much of an impact on a flat track in Wellington in the first Test.

So the last place was between Pigott and me. I kept staring at captain Bob Willis, anxious to know whether I was in the team or not but he seemed lost in thought as he proceeded to plonk his long legs (one at a time) on Thomas's shoulders in order to stretch his hamstrings. The uncertainty was gnawing away at me. We had finished the routine and I wondered where Bob was heading – was it in my direction? I needed to know. Eventually I saw him coming towards me and he told me I wasn't playing; as ever, Pigott had prevailed by a short head. Once again there was a mixture of emotions. I felt deflated at the prospect of another five days scurrying around in the dressing room and running errands, but there was also a scintilla of relief. This was not the appropriate reaction – there should have been no ambivalence at all and I should have been nothing but hugely disappointed – but the simple fact is that I wouldn't be put to the test now; I wouldn't fail. But I would be lumbered once more with those mind-numbing twelfth-man duties.

Not for long, however. In Christchurch England bowled badly and batted worse, posting 82 and 93 in their two completed innings, and we contrived to lose by an innings to New Zealand inside three days despite interruptions for rain. It would not have made any difference whether Pigott or Marks had occupied the final place. My selection for the next match in Auckland – a bore draw – did not turn the tide, and England lost a Test series against New Zealand for the first time.

I became all too accustomed to being one of the twelfth men on tour, where the duties would be shared by the non-players. In three winter tours, I experienced sixteen Tests, but only four of them as a player; then I would be let loose for the one-day internationals. Beyond the basic back-room chores and rushing out onto the field with drinks, hats, gloves and messages, there would occasionally be more unusual tasks. At Delhi in 1984, the dressing rooms were so far from the middle that the next batsman had to wait in a special section of the stand near the boundary to avoid an unacceptable delay after a wicket had fallen. So I was sent down to this area with this instruction: 'Go and talk to Gatt,' who was the next man in. I can't remember the topic of conversation.

During the closing stages of that game – and this was even more enjoyable than a chat with Gatt – I was summoned by Peter Baxter, the producer of the BBC's *Test Match Special*, to help him out in the commentary box since he had suddenly run out of summarizers. He knocked on the dressing-room door and wandered in while England were batting – as was possible on that tour – and said, 'I need someone to summa-rize. Anyone will do.' His other summarizers were either ill or attending a wedding, so I happily volunteered and therefore witnessed a special England victory in front of a microphone alongside Tony Lewis and Mike Carey, who was the *Daily Telegraph*'s correspondent at the time.

The Melbourne Boxing Day Test of 1982 produced a more stunning victory as England ended up winning by three runs after Geoff Miller had caught the ricochet from Chris Tavaré at second slip to dismiss Jeff Thomson, the last Australian batsman to fall. Throughout that game the quality of the English substitute fielders available was low, but we improvised shrewdly when it mattered – as Ian Gould, our reserve wicketkeeper, remembers in his autobiography. 'Graeme Fowler was struck on the toe by Thomson and couldn't field and the twelfth man options weren't great. Vic Marks wasn't much of an athlete; Jackers [Robin Jackman] could only do fine leg at both ends and Geoff Cook was struggling with a rib injury. That left me and I loved it.' That all tallies, I'm afraid. My recollection is that we happily bundled Ian out there since he was far keener to do it than anyone else – and better equipped. Before long he took a wonderful diving catch at cover to dismiss Australia's best batsman, Greg Chappell, off the bowling of Norman Cowans, which greatly enhanced England's chances of victory.

That was a decisive moment yet not quite so memorable as the dismissal of Australia's best batsman in 2005, Ricky Ponting. Australia were trying to stay in the fourth Test of the series at Trent Bridge. Damien Martyn pushed the ball defensively on the off side. Gary Pratt – a 23-year-old professional from Durham CCC, who was acting as England's twelfth man – swooped from cover: 'I just picked it up and hoped for the best.' The ball hit the base of the stumps and Ponting was 18 inches from home and furious – for many reasons: he was out; Martyn's call for a single had been a shocker but Ponting had not recognized the danger quickly enough; England had been abusing the system by using a twelfth man so liberally throughout the series (though on this occasion Simon Jones was properly injured and at the hospital while Pratt was on the field); the Ashes were slipping away. It was all too much for Ponting, and the Australian captain would be fined 75 per cent of his match fee for his outburst when leaving the field. Undoubtedly this was a seminal moment in the series and at the end of it a space was reserved for Pratt on the team bus that was driven around London in celebration. Suddenly Pratt was a household name and many still remember his run-out more than his fifty-three first-class appearances for Durham as a middle-order batsman.

Twelfth men rarely achieve such fame – though, in the case of Pratt, he grew frustrated that he was always associated with that throw from cover at Nottingham rather than his batting prowess. Usually they are doomed to the anonymity of a dogs-body. Now they even have to wear a bib (health and safety, I presume) as they sprint onto the grass at an international match. At least they have plenty of support staff back in the dressing room for some of the more menial tasks, which is not likely to be the case at county level. It was certainly not like that at Somerset in 1974, my first summer as a professional cricketer, when I had many days in the twelfth man's role.

There was no rest. You were obliged to bowl in the nets at around 10 a.m. to any batsman who wanted a hit to restore his confidence. I could fulfil that demand quite easily. Then the captain, Brian Close, needed a piping-hot pot of tea before the start of play and at every interval – he seemed to survive on tea plus twenty (or more) Benson & Hedges throughout every day of his gargantuan professional career. He might also need his twelfth man to pop down to the bookies to back a sure-fire winner on his behalf. With my sheltered background, I wasn't very good at this so I may have saved him a few bob. A swift visit to the fish and chip shop at lunchtime was often required. 'And don't forget to leave those tickets on the gate... and get me a packet of fags.'

Every dismissed batsman would expect a cold drink at his side upon return to the dressing room, a ritual rather than a necessity, and this could be a tricky operation. How to break the uncomfortable silence that accompanied such a swift return to the dressing room for one of my colleagues? 'Bad luck' was somehow not so appropriate after the batsman, who was probably keeping me out of the team, had advanced down the pitch, swung wildly towards mid-wicket just before hearing the death rattle.

Orders also had to be taken for the players' post-match drinks, which would consist mostly of pints of beer or lager, a dozen of which would be precariously balanced on a flimsy tray five minutes before the end of play, just as the corridors were packed with spectators leaving the ground or merrily pursuing their final drink of the day. Dropping this cargo on the way back to the dressing room could be a career-terminating moment. Then there was the job of running the communal bath early enough to ensure the hot water had not been snaffled by the away dressing room but late enough that it was still sufficiently hot to satisfy our brave warriors returning from the middle.

By contrast, going onto the field in place of an injured colleague was a doddle for the twelfth man. Back in the 1970s this might also mean fielding for the opposition as well. Visiting teams often travelled without a twelfth man to save money and manpower and there was the possibility of earning a few pounds if the opposition captain needed an emergency fielder because of an injury. Once, at Bournemouth, Somerset 'borrowed' Paul Terry, who was then an up-and-coming Hampshire batsman, doing the twelfth-man duties for the home side. Gordon Greenidge was at the crease and in full flow when Terry came on and was stationed at deep backward square leg. Greenidge was facing Hallam Moseley and he flicked the ball off his legs effortlessly from the meat of his bat and it sailed away; it seemed certain to clear the boundary until Terry dived like a swallow to take an astounding catch inches inside the rope. Greenidge c sub b Moseley 57. Terry didn't quite know where to sit at lunchtime but next to Greenidge was probably not a good option.

In the Parks when playing for Oxford University, I recall Leicestershire suffering from a spate of injuries and, since the University side did not have a twelfth man either, Martin Johnson, who was covering the match for the *Leicester Mercury*, was volunteered to go on the field as twelfth man by captain Ray Illingworth. Naturally, Johnson was stuck at short leg in those helmetless days and, in order to ingratiate himself with the pros, he even felt obliged to swear at one of our callow batsmen who was proving unusually obdurate. Johnson would have been quite good at that. I did not know him then but I came to enjoy his company many years later when he was working for the *Independent* newspaper and I had started writing for the *Observer*. If I had known him in the Parks I would have employed the sweep shot far more frequently against their spinners. That might have shut him up for a few minutes.

The canny young cricketer does not demonstrate how good

he is at short leg since this might result in him ending up there for great chunks of his career. By the same token, being an excellent twelfth man is not a reputation to pursue since you do not want to do this job too often either. But it is important for team morale to show willing; the unrelenting demands of the coach/captain must be satisfied. So a show of exuberant enthusiasm is required from the poor blighter who has just been left out of the team again. The futility of all this is often on display at our county grounds in the twenty-first century. I have witnessed a natural break in play after the first ball of the day when a batsman has been dismissed seconds after the start. Then what happens? A twelfth man rushes out onto the field, carrying a basket containing the individual drinks for all eleven players, and he offers them around for refreshment before sprinting off again. They have only been out there for two minutes.

This is probably a job for a fledging county pro rather than a senior player suffering the rare indignity of being left out of the team. Phil Edmonds was omitted from the Middlesex eleven in 1985 – at the age of 34 – so that they could play four seamers at Leicester two days after he had helped England win the Ashes at The Oval. 'I think they must be mad,' he said. The prospect of fulfilling the duties of the twelfth man did not appeal greatly to Edmonds and it is highly unlikely that he would have been a very good one. Servility does not come naturally to him. 'What benefit is there to anyone, Middlesex or me, to stay here in that capacity?' he said. Whereupon he got in his car and drove back to London. Middlesex won the match by ten wickets and went on to win the Championship.

10

Press Conferences

'... and the press box creaking, stretching,
fidgeting, vulture-like waits
with the sound of sharpening carbon claws
for the fresh carcass of play.'

John Snow (from 'Lord's Test' in
Moments and Thoughts, 1973)

'IT'S TOUGH BEING me' is a state of mind that most of us
have endured along the way, but not many have blurted this
out in front of the reporters of all our national newspapers.
However, Kevin Pietersen has – at Headingley in 2012 at the
end of the Test match against South Africa. He was the man
of the match, an obvious choice after striking a brilliant,
blistering 149 in England's first innings. This meant he was
obliged to speak to the press afterwards, an opportunity that
neither he nor his employers seemed to welcome very much.

Normally the post-match press conference was only of
passing interest to me. Here I had better make an admission:
I was never the most enthusiastic attendee of these occasions,
and very often there was a far more competent *Guardian*

journalist around – a David Hopps, Andy Wilson or Ali Martin – to assess what had been said at the press conference before reporting the best bits. Often the words delivered by the protagonists provided only mildly illuminating fare. At least, that was always my theory. But somehow, at Leeds on the evening of 5 August 2012, it fell upon me to do this duty for the *Guardian* and sadly it transpired that this press conference would not be a routine event. In a bizarre way it was, in fact, spellbinding. At the close of play after a hard-fought Test match, my main priority was to get on the road as swiftly as possible. It's a long way from Leeds to Exeter, where I live, so a brief résumé of the press conferences with a bit of rapid cutting and pasting would surely suffice.

Admittedly, it had been an eventful Test for an England side under pressure. They had lost the first match of the series to South Africa at The Oval by an innings and 12 runs, having taken only two wickets in the game. Here at Headingley the contest had ended as a draw but not until Pietersen had played a spectacular innings, Graeme Smith had made a surprising declaration and England had briefly flirted with an unlikely run chase by sending Pietersen out to open the batting in their second innings.

So, soon after stumps, I trotted down three flights of stairs from the press box and, with pad and pen in hand, I made my way into the press conference room. At one end of the room there was a small temporary stage and a couple of chairs behind a table packed with microphones and a variety of recording instruments that had just been placed there by the journalists. Facing that table, which had a portable backdrop displaying all the logos of the ECB's sponsors, were rows of chairs for the gentle men and women of the press, behind which a phalanx of photographers and cameramen were stationed, ready for the last action of a long day.

There were already murmurs as the press corps congregated. Something was up. Pietersen had just given a live interview on the outfield to Jonathan Agnew, the BBC's cricket correspondent, and towards the end of their exchange he had acknowledged the possibility that the Lord's Test – the next and final one in the series – might be his last for England. As you would expect, the newshounds were on to that. This was a very strange thing for the man of the match, who had recently blitzed the ball all around Headingley, to say. Some sort of explanation was required.

Everyone shuffled swiftly into place as a stern-faced Pietersen marched into the room, staring into the middle distance, accompanied only by the ECB's press officer, Rhian Evans. This entrance aroused further curiosity. Usually the captain and the man of the match give a joint press conference at the end of a Test match, but there was no sign of the England captain, Andrew Strauss. Once Pietersen was seated he mumbled, 'I'm not waiting for Strauss. I've got to get on the road.' Well, Kevin and I now had something in common. The assembled press corps, with John Etheridge of *The Sun* and Stephen Brenkley of the *Independent* to the fore, tried to find out what was behind Pietersen's odd remarks to Agnew.

'I won't elaborate,' Pietersen said, dutifully wearing the correct sponsor's baseball cap. (Who said he was unmanageable?) 'You can ask me a hundred times but I'm not saying anything until after the Lord's Test.'

He stuck to this response for the next half a dozen questions. The experienced hacks knew they should keep plugging away. In earlier, more uncomplicated times, Ray Illingworth or David Lloyd, when they were in charge of the England team, might have protested that discretion was their middle name, but the journos learned to keep them talking. Both were innately garrulous; sometimes both of them revelled in the ridiculous theatre of a press conference. Keep them talking and they would say something they meant to keep to themselves, something that might lead tomorrow's column. So now the press kept KP talking and, while he did not deliver a revelation or even an explanation, he said more than enough. Recently he had been in talks with the ECB about his future, having previously announced that he was retiring from ODI cricket. Those talks, he assured us, were 'absolutely not about money'. The more determined he was to try to say nothing, the wider the gulf between Pietersen and the ECB seemed to be. It wasn't just about his schedule or his need to spend more time with his family. And he kept insisting it was certainly not about the money. He made it crystal clear that he was unhappy that the content of his talks with the ECB earlier in the summer had been leaked. 'Did I leak anything? Not for a second... never a single word.' This was the first time he had become animated in the press conference. His defences were cracking.

But what we all remembered that night – and indeed almost a decade later – was his response to a seemingly innocent question (it is often the seemingly innocent question that gets the most striking response) about how much his fans would miss him if he stopped playing Test cricket. Initially he stuck to his script: 'You'll find out more soon enough.' But then he could not resist adding, 'The saddest part is that there are spectators out there who love watching me play.' It would be 'a huge shame' if he did not continue playing Test cricket. Then came 'It's tough being me, playing for England.'

'It's tough being me.' That was the phrase that struck home, that highlighted Pietersen's cauldron of confusion and despair. 'That line has haunted me ever since,' he wrote in his autobiography a few years later. No matter that it was tough for all the England players, especially the less gifted ones, who now included the debutant at Headingley, James Taylor, who would later recall how Pietersen had belittled him at a pre-Test net session with a dismissive 'What are you doing here?'

Pietersen, who had flayed the South African bowlers without any inhibitions a couple of days before, was in some turmoil. He could not hide his feelings any longer. Clearly he was fed up with his employers and some of his peers even if we did not hear the detail that night. Yet, amid the confusion and despair, he had played the most astounding innings in this Test match. It now seemed as if he was only content in the haven that was the middle, the one place where he could be in charge of his own destiny as a ball was propelled in his direction at about 90 mph; perhaps the only other happy place was in his own home miles from any of his colleagues. For a high-profile international cricketer constantly under the spotlight, the dressing room was always supposed to be the safe refuge but that was obviously no longer the case for Pietersen.

Only the truly great players appear able to excel while beset with seemingly insurmountable off-field distractions. The pitch becomes their natural habitat, where they are most relaxed. In 2005, during the greatest ever Test series, Shane Warne had some major complications in his personal life, yet throughout that summer he was quite brilliant out on the field, taking 40 Test wickets and scoring 249 runs. By the Oval Test match the 'Where's your missus gone?' chant had given way to 'There's only one Shane Warne.' Geoffrey Boycott has never been more relaxed than when booted and padded at the crease. He was at ease there and in charge of his life; it was where he truly belonged. This was now true of Pietersen.

The press conference came to an end. As he was leaving, Pietersen apparently said to Rhian Evans, 'Well, that went pretty well, I think.' That may have been a hasty conclusion and it was not necessarily one shared by the England camp or his agent, Adam Wheatley, whose immediate response was, 'This could create some serious shit.' Maybe Pietersen was relieved that the press had not asked him about the texts he had sent to the South African players, an issue that was soon to hit the headlines. As he left the room, in came Strauss, wondering aloud what his teammate had just said, though it actually suited him not to know as he set about answering his questions. The Strauss press conference could not match the drama of its predecessor. We have all forgotten it by now.

I have checked it out and he was obviously keen to retain a veneer of unity. 'He [KP] is an unbelievable player in great form. Team unity has been outstanding over the last three years and will continue to be so.' This was Strauss the politician, saying the right thing and, as we would soon find out, clutching at straws.

So I climbed back up the stairs into the press box, where I made an unusual call, telephoning the *Guardian* sports desk, which I rarely did at this time of day. I may have had a reputation there of downplaying the odd controversy. Indeed, their impression may well have been that news stories were regarded by me as a nasty inconvenience, an occupational hazard, to be avoided wherever possible. In which case, they were probably right. Where were Hopps, Wilson or Martin when I needed them?

One Saturday night in St John's Wood two years earlier, when England were playing Pakistan, might confirm that impression. I was having a drink with Jonathan Agnew after the day's play at Lord's and it became apparent that the BBC's news desk was ringing him urgently about a possible scam in the Test match involving Mohammad Amir, the 18-year-old Pakistan paceman who had bowled an outrageous no-ball earlier in the day. Apparently the *News of the World* had a bit of a story. Being the dutiful reporter, I rang my office at around 9 p.m. to explain the hazy details that had come my way, if only to ensure that they kept an eye on the first editions of the Sunday papers. Just before I finished the call, I remember saying, 'I thought I'd better let you know but I don't suppose it will amount to much.' They soon rang back, my drink had to be swallowed swiftly and I hurried off to my room to open the laptop again.

At Leeds, to my dismay, I had to tell the office that we had not witnessed a routine post-match press conference. More space would be required and more time would have to elapse before I could point my car southwards. The next half-hour in the press box disappeared as the keyboard on my laptop was battered. There were deadlines to meet, those of the paper and the self-imposed ones that might help me to get home before 2 a.m. There was not much time for thinking. 'Seldom has a man of the match looked so glum,' I said before sprinting to the bottom of the page as rapidly as possible with plenty of Pietersen quotes along the way.

I eventually set off for Devon with two contrasting thoughts in my mind. Clearly quite a story was brewing (though at this point I was unaware of Pietersen texting his old mates in the South African dressing room). And on the following day I was off to Paris for the first time in my life, where my wife's birthday could be celebrated. It was all booked up and all booked out with the paper. An absolutely dedicated, self-important journo might have insisted on cancelling the holiday to enable those vital, definitive pieces on the Pietersen saga to be delivered to eager readers. Needless to say, such a thought did not enter my head. Instead I packed my bag with a spring in my step, hoping that the little hotel near the Eiffel Tower would come somewhere close to expectations while remaining intrigued how my *Guardian* colleagues would deal with the inevitable rumpus. We had a good time exploring Paris but while I was there I did, at least, keep an eye on the *Guardian* website for Pietersen developments. From the banks of the Seine, it seemed as if the cricketing world had lost its marbles.

By the time I was required to burst into print a week later, it was just two days before the Lord's Test and a lot had changed. Everyone now knew about the Pietersen texts if not their precise content. Lexicographers had debated the meaning of the Afrikaans word 'doos'. Meanwhile, the details of the 'KP Genius' parody Twitter account had become public knowledge even to sensible Neanderthals like myself who had remained determined to shun Twitter. And Pietersen had been dropped from the Test team for the final match of the series at Lord's. All this while I had been pottering up and down the Seine, gazing at Monet's water lilies and marvelling at the buttresses of Notre-Dame. Upon my return, I had to admit to my readers that I'd been on holiday, before suggesting that distance can sometimes lend perspective. By now the parody Twitter account had been closed down. Of course it had. There was no point in it any more; real life had long since transcended parody. I wrote that Pietersen, even though he must be incredibly difficult to manage, would still be in my team at Lord's. I think this was the minority view among the press corps.

Of course, Pietersen was not the first cricketer to express reservations about his captain. This has been commonplace since the days of Grace. As Peter Roebuck once observed, 'Captaincy seems to involve half-hearing conversations which you'd rather not hear at all.' It is safe to assume that Mike Denness was seldom praised to the skies by Geoffrey Boycott in the 1970s. Dennis Lillee was not a great admirer of Kim Hughes's leadership skills and he rarely kept that a secret. Shane Warne, in private or public, rarely dwelt upon the virtues of John Buchanan, Australia's coach. Even the good captains get slagged off sometimes; this was an occupational hazard for Ray Illingworth, Mike Brearley, Nasser Hussain and now Andrew Strauss. It happens all the time to the bad ones.

I concluded by looking ahead to the Lord's Test, 'Victory for England and the management will be hailed as miracle workers. And defeat? Well, it will probably be Pietersen's fault.' England lost by 51 runs.

It was striking during that Headingley press conference how Pietersen was left to swim – or sink – on his own. There was no intervention from the ECB beyond a 'two more questions' from Rhian Evans even though it was obvious that Pietersen was, to borrow from his agent, 'creating some serious shit'. In his book Pietersen explains that he did not want to do the press conference but was told there was no choice: 'Andy Flower should have pulled me away from that or somebody should have controlled the questions and saved me from myself.'

That criticism certainly did not apply at the next press conference I attended when Pietersen was centre stage. This one took place in Colombo on 3 October 2012 – two months after the Headingley Test – and it was carefully, preposterously orchestrated. Pietersen was in Sri Lanka, working as a pundit for ESPN at the T20 World Cup, having been omitted from an England squad that, in his absence, failed to make the semifinals. He did not have so much to say on this occasion. For most of the time he sat in grim-faced silence and a sober, grey suit while Giles Clarke, the chairman of the ECB, did most of the talking. There had been some sort of rapprochement between the warring parties, though this was not discernible from the look on their faces. Pietersen had apologized for something but, since it was now agreed that those texts were merely 'provocative' rather than 'derogatory', it was tricky to establish exactly what. Then there was much talk of a tortuous 'reintegration process' that would be overseen by the England team's head coach, Andy Flower. In an old-fashioned way I could only suggest that in another era the protagonists would have taken themselves off to the nearest bar until they were 'as reintegrated as parrots', after which they might have buried some of their hatchets.

Eventually there was an opportunity for questions – three of them, to be precise – in an ECB operation that was desperately trying to leave nothing to chance. Two were allocated to Sky TV and *The Times* and, just to break the Murdoch monopoly, one was given to the *Daily Mail*. So much for glasnost.

The reintegration process may have been marginally more successful than that of Neville Chamberlain, but it did not last for ever. Pietersen returned to the England team and would play sixteen more Tests, hitting a brilliant century against India in Mumbai in November 2012 and another against Australia in Manchester the following summer. His last match was the Sydney Test of January 2014, after which there was more aggro and more confusion – especially when Colin Graves, now the chairman of the ECB, independently tossed out the notion that perhaps Pietersen could, after all, return to the England set-up following some good performances for Surrey in the County Championship. By now Strauss, who must have grimaced when he heard the comments of his chairman, was the ECB's director of cricket; despite Graves's intervention, there was no way back for Pietersen.

The Pietersen affair generated more vitriol – from both sides of the argument – than any other issue in my time involved in cricket. In part this is because in the twenty-first century there are far more vehicles for vitriol, which is often delivered with cowardly anonymity. I missed much of it by shunning Twitter, but even below the line on the *Guardian* website there was some shocking stuff. The moderators could not rest easily. Pietersen must have been extraordinarily difficult to play with, but over the years there has been a pattern of antipathy in the press to an outsider coming in, so he had few allies there. To a lesser extent Tony Greig, Allan Lamb, Graeme Hick and Andy Caddick endured that as well.

Pietersen was also a sensational player, which is why I always tended to be in favour of selecting him. (I have this weakness for wanting to play the best team.) He waltzes into the top five English batsmen in the half a century or so that I have been looking on, sitting easily alongside (not in order of merit but in a notional batting order) Geoff Boycott, Graham Gooch, David Gower and Joe Root. None of them could have surpassed the innings Pietersen played at The Oval in 2005 or the three centuries in Colombo, Headingley and Mumbai in 2012. No wonder there was some mystification during that year about Pietersen's life being so tough.

I have been to some press conferences not involving Pietersen. Many of them have been forgotten. Sometimes it was more instructive to listen to the questions. The most potent were often the shortest and most innocent of enquiries, which would usually be delivered by the tabloid journalists. They were more likely to produce a little bit of dynamite. At the other end of the spectrum would be the showboating question, more often from one of the broadsheets, where the main purpose seemed to be to display the wit and erudition of the questioner rather than to elicit some fresh insight from the player. All very entertaining but of no use at all.

Some of the Test captains could be very impressive. Australia's Mark Taylor would always give a good conference and, since his side was usually in the ascendancy, he could adopt the tone of a down-to-earth university lecturer who was willing and able to explain some of the finer points to any eager students listening in. John Wright of New Zealand could be disarmingly candid, as was the case after New Zealand had just lost a Test match at Edgbaston in 1990. 'Putting them into bat? It was just a terrible decision. All my fault,' he said – an assessment rarely reached by other Test captains after a disappointing defeat.

My predecessors have told me how Tony Greig (leaving aside his expressed determination to make the West Indies 'grovel' in 1976) and Mike Brearley understood the system well. In *The Art of Captaincy* Brearley admits 'enjoying' his press conferences even if England had just lost. Both recognized that, with a little forethought, they could dictate the content of the conversation and therefore the reporting of the press conference by tossing out some unlikely, newsy notion that might distract from more uncomfortable subjects. Among the next generation of England captains Nasser Hussain was the most adept at this.

M. S. Dhoni was just as calm and objective once the match was over as he was on the pitch. On one occasion he invited an interrogator to join him on the stage to discuss India's plight and, amid much merriment, he managed to do this without humiliating the startled journalist. He could be insightful too. His post-series analysis of India's defeat to England in 2012, where he highlighted how Monty Panesar had had such an impact because he spun the ball at such a rapid pace compared to the other spinners in the series, was a case in point.

After the West Indies' World T20 victory over England in Kolkata in 2016, Marlon Samuels did not really have to say anything at his press conference; he demonstrated that he was pretty pleased with life – and himself – just in the way that he plonked his feet on the table in front of him as if lying on a sofa (a pose imitated by Jacob Rees-Mogg to lesser effect on the front bench of the House of Commons in 2019). In the meantime his captain, Darren Sammy, thanked God for their victory and Mark Nicholas, who had described the West Indies as 'brainless' in an article for Cricinfo before the tournament began, thus providing another great incentive for Sammy's team to prevail. This gave me the opportunity to warn my readers not to get the two recipients of Sammy's gratitude confused.

Inzamam ul-Haq, when captain of Pakistan, was usually less forthcoming. In Faisalabad on the eve of a Test match against England, he would have a net and then spend most of the time reclining in a wicker chair on the outfield. At some point he would give a pre-match press conference from there, which would reveal very little – unless his interpreter was guilty of a massive revision of his comments. As we were all leaving the outfield there was mumbling about Inzamam delivering 'much Urdu about nothing' again, an observation I naturally stole and popped into my copy the next day.

Some captains, like Virat Kohli, could be spiky; others gave the impression they would rather be somewhere else. Mike Atherton – now the consummate journalist – was sometimes one of those. He would be amenable to the broadsheets but distant and occasionally disdainful to the tabloids, which lost him a few friends at the start of his long reign as England captain. But when necessary he could deliver a fine conference, such as the one after England had just been bowled out for 46 in Trinidad in 1994. The survival instinct usually kicks in when necessary. Once he had crossed to the other side, Atherton became a hugely accomplished and popular member of the press and commentary boxes. Soon he was the person required to ask the questions rather than answer them. With microphone in hand, he was given the job of conducting those post-match ceremonies with the captains. Early on in his TV career he was interviewing Stephen Fleming, then the urbane and very capable captain of New Zealand. Atherton asked his question and Fleming paused thoughtfully before eventually replying 'Yes' followed by... nothing else. Experienced onlookers could spot the panic in Atherton's eyes and the twinkle in Fleming's. The novice interviewer needed more than that... and he needed another question fast. The disappointment for the voyeurs was the fact that Fleming, being such a reasonable man, eventually showed compassion and began to answer Atherton's long-forgotten question at some length. A few of us thought he could have remained silent a little longer.

Generally the conferences after a cricketing calamity are well attended and more interesting, which meant there was a fair chance I'd be there. Bizarrely it is reckoned that the press conference after England had been bowled out for 51 in Jamaica in 2009, which was delivered around the pool of the team's hotel the morning after the match, catapulted Andy Flower into the role of permanent head coach. At the time he was in temporary charge and he delivered such an earnest, considered performance with some of his employers like cricket director, Hugh Morris, hovering in the background that he emerged as a stronger candidate for the full-time job despite England's recent capitulation at Sabina Park.

Sometimes press conferences can provide drama that embraces both farce and hubris, and the best examples recently have been provided by Steve Smith and Cameron Bancroft of Australia. First there was the hilarious account given by Bancroft after the Brisbane Test in November 2017 of being greeted by Jonny Bairstow in a Perth bar at the start of that Ashes tour by a headbutt (non-malicious). This was a source of great amusement for the assembled press corps of both countries but no one was as amused as Steve Smith, the Australian captain, who was doubled up and incapable of speech at Bancroft's side as the tale unfolded. In that account Bairstow was vindicated (because it became apparent that there was no malice in his greeting) but he was also ridiculed ruthlessly. Bancroft gave a bravura performance as he recounted the meeting with the English team just after they had arrived in the country four weeks earlier. It is still hard to work out whether this was a calculated performance by Bancroft, brilliantly delivered, or simply his natural retelling of a bizarre greeting ritual. The generous view is the latter. But there was something sinister about this topic being picked up on the stump microphone via a few words from David Warner a month later at the Gabba and then all too eagerly made public. The Australians seized their chance to undermine an England tour, which was already faltering badly. An Ashes contest now goes beyond runs and wickets; there is the propaganda war to win as well.

The England tourists and their management team, who had just endured defeat in the first Test of the series, were not amused; they were furious. One of their key men had been made to look stupid and the general behaviour of the touring party was now under even more extreme scrutiny. Bear in mind that this took place against the backdrop of the Ben Stokes incident in Bristol in September 2016, which had ended with Stokes omitted from the tour party and suspicions rife of a drinking culture within the England set-up. So this 'hilarious' episode caused significant damage to England on that tour. The headbutt story was not a random event even if we accept that the tenor of Bancroft's retelling of the story was not premeditated. At that post-match press conference, the sight of Steve Smith laughing uncontrollably at the humiliation of a fellow professional cricketer was ugly and inappropriate.

Then came an example of hubris that would interest the Greek tragedians of the classical era. In March 2018 there was another press conference in Cape Town and this time Steve Smith was not laughing, though one or two of the England players, who were engaged upon a tour of New Zealand at the time, could not hide a smile or two. Look at the photos: the faces of Smith and Bancroft were the living embodiment of desolation. Not only were they made to look stupid – like Bairstow – but in time they were shown to be dishonest. Preposterous though this may seem, Smith and his sidekicks soon contrived to have something in common with President Nixon after the break-in at the Watergate Office Building in 1972: it was the attempted cover-up that did for them.

Suddenly Smith, David Warner and, to a lesser extent, Bancroft, were pariahs in their own country. No punishment was severe enough for them as prime ministers of Australia and the UK, attempting to seize the mood of the nation, blundered in. Then Smith burst into tears and the pendulum of public opinion swung again in Australia. Looking on from afar, I was aghast. How could Australians seriously believe that, while the cricketers of other nations had in the past, in a dastardly fashion, tried to tamper with a cricket ball, this was an activity that would never have been undertaken by any of their own players? There was another strand to this furore, which was just as important. Everyone, even a fair proportion of Australians, were fed up with the bullying arrogance of some of their cricketers – and here they were caught trying to cheat oh so clumsily. They got Al Capone on taxes and the Australian cricket team on ball-tampering. This was a crazy affair that provoked a crazy reaction – and also a few press conferences that were mesmerizing.

Some of these gatherings are more innocent. During England's last Test of their tour to South Africa in 2019/20, I was sitting next to Scyld Berry in what would be his final match as a cricket correspondent after more than forty years in harness (though he had assured us that he would still be writing about cricket for the *Telegraph* on a regular basis thereafter). The match finished in a rush and, as ever, there was a flurry of activity in the press and commentary boxes. This is always a frantic time. Nick Hoult – the omni-capable *Telegraph* man who would succeed Scyld as correspondent – came over just before the end of the match and, to my surprise, began to beseech his old colleague to join him at the post-match press conferences. 'There will be so many people put up after the game. I need some help over there,' he pleaded. This struck me as very strange. Nick was/is the consummate journo, who would normally deal with such tasks in the blink of an eye. He has been adept at ghosting Geoffrey Boycott, Shane Warne and Kevin Pietersen as well as knocking up a news piece – all on the same day if necessary – yet here he was, almost begging his senior correspondent to join him in the tiresome but essential mopping-up of quotes. I began to wonder whether I should offer my services at the press conference to my colleague at the *Guardian* (a noble notion, swiftly abandoned). Berry agreed to join Hoult at the press conference with the minimum of fuss, which slightly surprised me. Before long I understood why: Hoult had to get his colleague into the dungeon of the press conference room at the Wanderers somehow because at the end of proceedings the England captain, Joe Root, wanted to make a presentation (of a cricket print) to mark the last Test to be covered by Berry as a correspondent. And so he did. It was, I'm told – and I've seen the pictures of a beaming Berry – a warm and uplifting moment and, with hindsight, another press conference that I should have attended. They are not always a self-serving exercise in cynicism.

However, 2020 was probably a record year for me in terms of attending press conferences. The main reason for this was that because of the Covid pandemic they were all conducted on Zoom, whether the journalists were sitting in their favourite armchair at home or in the press box at the ground. Throughout the entire summer the press and players were kept well apart yet the lines of communication were arguably more open than they had ever been – in part thanks to Danny Reuben, the best media manager the ECB have had. Canny Danny manages to understand the needs of the press corps and retain the confidence of the players simultaneously, which is a trickier operation than you might think. He initiated countless media opportunities despite the restrictions of 2020. Moreover, during the Test matches, players were made available for interview on Sky TV during the match as well as in their Zoom conferences after the close of play. Once again this was a mutually beneficial operation; the TV audience enjoyed the interviews while those players nearing the end of their careers had an opportunity to demonstrate how invaluable they might be in the commentary box in the not-too-distant future.

Two interviews – one on Sky, one via Zoom – stood out, both of them from England's senior citizens, Stuart Broad and Jimmy Anderson, who demonstrated that they had learned a bit about media management over the years. After being omitted from the first Test against the West Indies at the Ageas Bowl, Broad gave a candid interview to Sky that immediately demanded attention. 'I'm not a particularly emotional person but I've found the last couple of days quite tough,' he said. 'To say I'm disappointed would be an understatement. You only get disappointed if you drop your phone and break the screen. I've been frustrated, angry, gutted – because it's quite a hard decision to understand. I've probably bowled the best I've ever bowled in the last couple of years. I felt like it was my shirt, having been in the team through the Ashes and going to South Africa and winning there.'

Broad trod the line brilliantly, as did those who had made the decision to leave him out. He received no criticism from the England hierarchy for his strong reaction to being dropped. Instead they applauded his response since they reasoned that it reflected his hunger to keep playing for England. Broad's anger was now a good-news story, as reflected by Jimmy Anderson later in the day. 'I think you're fully aware he [Broad] has not taken it very well. And I think it's great for the team because it shows that he's passionate and he's desperate to be part of our success.' In Broad's absence, England had surprisingly lost that Test match against the West Indies so there was no way they could avoid bringing him back into the team for the next one. For the rest of the summer he was in brilliant form. He had talked the talk and then he walked the walk – the trickier bit – quite superbly. Meanwhile, the England set-up had managed to make a virtue of Broad sharing his dismay so openly.

Something similar happened after the first Test against Pakistan in 2020. This time Anderson was behind the microphone on a Zoom call in between Tests. By his very high standards, he had just produced a poor Test performance. Now, like Broad, he was unusually candid albeit not quite so forthright as his partner. 'It's been a frustrating week for me,' he said. 'I've not bowled very well and felt out of rhythm. For the first time in probably ten years I got a little bit emotional on the field. In the second innings in particular, a chance went down and I let it get to me. I just felt I wasn't bowling to the standards I set myself. It reminded me of when I first started playing. When you get frustrated and a little bit angry you try and bowl quicker and quicker and it doesn't help. Now I'll just try to work hard and hope I get the nod for the next game.'

Somehow there was a subtext, as Anderson scotched any thoughts of an imminent retirement. It was 'I'm desperate to play; I'm fit to play; I'm ready to play. You'd better pick me.' Which they did, and he bowled much better in the next match. He knew it would have been hard to leave him out after that interview. So Broad and Anderson are now canny operators off the field as well as on it. In Anderson's case this represents quite a change. When he started playing for England in 2002 he was painfully shy. Now in an understated way he seems to enjoy the odd press conference.

Indeed, I've often been puzzled why players should regard giving a press conference as a chore. For those not burdened by the captaincy, it usually represents an opportunity to explain to a captive audience how it was that you came to perform so well out on the field. It offers a stage that I would have liked to experience rather more frequently in my playing career. In my view, it is better to give press conferences than to receive them – unless you have something to hide.

11

The Library

'The Don, it appears, had two views of bouncers – one
when they were bowled against him and the other
when bowled by his side with no fear of retaliation.'

Jack Fingleton, *Batting from Memory*, 1946

OVER THE YEARS I have acquired a lot of cricket books. The
shelves I'm staring at are full of them, some of the best ever
written on the game and some of the worst (inevitably, it is
the review copies in this category that come rushing through
the post). When downsizing I'll have to get rid of many of
them; during the lockdowns I have thought about organizing
them but this has yet to happen. How should I sort them? By
alphabet, chronology, size, colour? There might be another
way. I have always had a tendency to shy away from conflict
whenever possible. I'm not sure this is a virtue but it is a fact.
Yet maybe I could become more provocative, more confronta-
tional as I get older – in the arrangement of my cricket books.

There is *The Art of Cricket* by Don Bradman, first published in 1958. 'It is brilliant,' says Richie Benaud in the

preface of one of the reprints. It is also pragmatic, which comes as no great surprise. Bradman was obviously a genius but he was a pragmatic genius. Early on in the book there is a piece of advice that even the old MCC coaching manual has over-looked. In a section entitled 'Shoes and Socks' he writes, 'It is wise to keep the boots in a small linen bag. In this way dirt off the shoes will not soil your clothes.' Ma Bradman hits the spot.

Among his peers Bradman was not the most popular cricketer ever to play for Australia and he was not the sort of skipper who was likely to sort out any problem in the team over a beer in the bar after play, which might well have been Ian Chappell's preference a few decades later. Bradman liked to plough his own furrow once stumps were drawn – sometimes in his room, meticulously responding to a massive mailbag. This was his natural inclination but it also became a policy decision. 'When the captain is bent upon a good time his team-mates quickly find out and there is a resultant deterioration in morale and discipline,' he says at the start of the chapter on captaincy. Ian Botham and Freddie Flintoff must have skipped that one.

But whom should I place next to Bradman? We could put Bill O'Reilly's autobiography, *Tiger*, there since these two teammates famously never got on. 'You could say we did not like each other, but it would be closer to the truth to say we chose to have little to do with each other,' O'Reilly wrote in his autobiography. 'Bradman was a teetotaller, ambitious, conservative and meticulous. I was outspoken and gregari-ous, an equally ambitious young man of Irish descent.' Here O'Reilly does not focus upon the Catholic/Protestant divide that is often mentioned when discussing the tensions within the Australian teams of that era. But the truth is I do not possess a copy of this book, which is a pity since O'Reilly was not only an accomplished, aggressive wrist-spinner of the highest quality in Australian sides captained by Bradman, he was also an accomplished and aggressive writer about the game. Sadly the same applies with *Batting From Memory*, a book by Jack Fingleton, another teammate who never threatened to be Bradman's closest associate. Instead it is tempting to emulate the arrangement in the Long Room at Lord's for many years, when a portrait of Douglas Jardine was hung alongside one of the Don. In this instance we could place Christopher Douglas's *Douglas Jardine, Spartan Cricketer* alongside *The Art of Cricket* on the shelves. And on the other side Duncan Hamilton's excellent biography of Harold Larwood might sit very nicely.

On the Bodyline tour of 1932/33 Jardine instructed his players to refer to Australia's star batsman not as 'Bradman' or 'The Don' but as 'the little bastard'. This may not have been a hardship for some of the players in the England tour party. Larwood liked Australians but there is little evidence that he liked Bradman much. Even though he emigrated to Sydney, he only met Bradman four times after the Bodyline tour and on one occasion this was a purely random and very brief meeting in the streets of his adopted city.

In time the vast majority of Australians also liked Larwood as he lived out his later years in increasing anonymity in the Sydney suburbs. Occasionally there would be visitors – pilgrims almost – especially when England were touring.

These included the inimitable *Guardian* sports journalist and renowned pipe smoker, Frank Keating, in 1993 when Larwood, now 88 years of age, had just about lost his sight. As ever, Keating wrote memorably about the occasion: 'On the mantelpiece is a small silver ashtray. I tap my pipe out on it. The old man hears a clink. "I think you've just emptied your ash in my most treasured possession," he says, though without any trace of admonition. "Read what it says," he orders. You read: "To Harold. For The Ashes. From a Grateful Skipper."'

Larwood would probably not be Bradman's choice of neighbour. Of great English bowlers, he would have preferred Alec Bedser with whom he became friendly towards the end of his playing career and for years to come. After touring Australia just after the Second World War, Bedser wrote to Bradman, asking for some bowling tips. 'It did seem to me that the best ball you bowled was the one which went away to the slips off the pitch and if you could reproduce for instance the one with which you bowled me in Adelaide then you would not have to worry about any others,' replied Bradman in a typed letter from his office at an Adelaide investment brokers. From there their friendship blossomed and they regularly exchanged letters – handwritten and warm – over the next fifty years.

There have been several tantalizing feuds in cricket but perhaps not as many as we might expect, given how long players are together on tour, in dressing rooms and, in recent times, the confines of the team hotel during yet another lockdown. Somehow the game is more likely to create a bond between cricketers of varying backgrounds and outlooks rather than impenetrable barriers. Likewise, most of the feuds are eventually settled or at least laid to rest in the end. Even so, there is scope for a little more mischief on the bookshelves.

There are a few contenders to place next to *KP*, the bestselling autobiography of Kevin Pietersen. It is tempting go with Andrew Strauss's *Driving Ambition* on one side and Graeme Swann's *The Breaks are Off* on the other. (Somehow I do not seem to have a copy of Matt Prior's autobiography, inevitably entitled *The Gloves are Off*, which would also be worth considering as a neighbour for *KP*, given how scathing Pietersen was about Prior in his book.)

This is where a good index becomes invaluable. There is a well-established ritual upon the launch of a new cricket book: on picking up a copy still fresh from the printers, the trigger movement is to go straight to the index to look for your name; if it's there, the urge to flick to the relevant page numbers and to check what the combination of ghostwriter and cricketer have written about you is irresistible. There may be the odd flicker of disappointment if you're not there, since we all know there's only one thing worse than being talked about. The ideal balance for a successful autobiography is to deliver enough spice to satisfy the salacious demands of those who might want to offer a lucrative contract for serializations in a newspaper or glossy magazine but not enough to make too many of your old colleagues lifelong enemies. This is a tricky undertaking, which I've yet to master.

We will have to put Mike Brearley's seminal work *The Art of Captaincy* (or any other of his more recent offerings) alongside Simon Barnes's *A Singular Man*, a biography of Phil Edmonds that was published in 1986. During their careers

Brearley and Edmonds, by mutual consent, often failed to bring out the best in one another. Any suggestion that their arguments were just cricket-related – a few petty disagreements on tactics – does not hold water. It was more than that but hardly a feud. In Barnes's book Edmonds sought to be contrite but he couldn't quite manage it. 'I see now that I should have made efforts to be nice, sensible and rational and to get along with him, to establish a harmonious working relationship. When he asked me to slog for bonus points [at Middlesex] after he had batted 70 overs for 70 I should have said "Certainly, Brears" instead of getting uptight and asking him "Is this a team game or what?"'

In fact, Edmonds points out that he was something of an ally for Brearley in the early days at Middlesex when the old pro brigade in the Lord's dressing room were resentful of their new county captain and their fading grip on the dressing room. Yet both Brearley and Edmonds acknowledge that, in the end, they were not always good for one another in their later years.

Edmonds was – and still is, I imagine – a remarkably single-minded character, who may be alone in thinking that Geoffrey Boycott was a better captain than Brearley. Edmonds does not quite say that in his book, but he recognizes that he bowled better for Boycott than he did for Brearley when playing for England: 'All I know is that when Boycott took over [after Brearley's arm was broken] I got 7-66 in the third Test in Karachi [on the 1977/78 tour of Pakistan and New Zealand].' These were Edmonds's best figures in Test cricket. Brearley does not disagree with this thesis. He writes in *The Art of Captaincy*, 'He [Edmonds] felt, I think rightly, that he would have done better with his own Zambian upbringing with a more extrovert, abrasive, physically tough captain like Ian Chappell. Possibly Geoff Boycott got more out of him than I could. I noticed that Edmonds reacted well to Boycott's jibes in the nets. Each time he bowled a bad ball Boycott would leer at him, saying "Another fower!"'

Somehow the presence of Boycott at mid-off giving some of his blunt Yorkshire common sense seemed to enhance Edmonds, a bowler easily bored. Edmonds also bowled very well for another England captain, who is not often lauded to the skies, David Gower. On the 1984/85 tour of India – a triumphant one for England – Edmonds was the linchpin of Gower's attack even though he lost his (very short) run-up throughout most of the series. On that tour Edmonds's eccentricities – which included drawn curtains whatever the time of day or night, and the BBC World Service constantly at full volume on the radio – were tolerated. Additionally, at the various official functions attended by the team – and there were quite a lot in those days – he provided us all with a reliable indication of who was the most important person in the room. Edmonds would be talking to him/her within five minutes of our arrival.

Neither Boycott nor Gower felt threatened by Edmonds's considerable ego. Boycott was not bothered by that. He even started calling Edmonds and himself 'The Fitzwilliam boys' since Edmonds was a student at Fitzwilliam College in Cambridge while Boycott was born at Fitzwilliam in Yorkshire. Meanwhile, Gower knew that his left-arm spinner was indebted to him for bringing him back from the wilderness.

Besides, perhaps Gower had some sympathy with the noncon-formist in the outer ring; in his gentle way he would become one himself.

So Edmonds is one of the very few cricketers not to be enhanced by Brearley's captaincy. However, many years after they have hung up their boots, I imagine they could co-exist easily enough on the shelves. Or I could put Edmonds along-side one of Boycott's books like *The Corridor of Certainty* (at least they found a good title effortlessly enough). But there are other contenders for that slot.

Fred Trueman: The Authorised Biography by Chris Waters surely has to be there. Part of the book charts the background of the internecine wars of the 1970s and 1980s in Yorkshire cricket and how Trueman and Boycott were not on speaking terms for a couple of decades. In his 1987 autobiography Boycott says, 'Trueman waged a systematic and virtually unbroken campaign of character assassination against me' [often via his column in the *People*]. But in early 2003 Trueman – to the astonishment of many, including members of his own family – rang Boycott up. His son, Rodney, was taken aback when Fred said he was going to see him. 'Dad, you've spent all my childhood hating Geoff Boycott and now you're going to see him?'

'Well, he's got cancer now – that's different,' replied Fred.

Waters' book starts brilliantly with a 'last supper' scene (though it was actually lunch): a reunion of Fred, who was late, Brian Close and Ray Illingworth, a trio who never really fell out with one another despite inhabiting a tempestuous – and very successful – dressing room together, and Boycott, who fell out with all three of them at various times in his career. Now

Boycott speaks warmly of Fred as well as the other two giants of Yorkshire cricket.

Boycott also recalls his fertile relationship with Bob Barber, his first opening partner for England. Barber brooked no nonsense from the start. He had never met Boycott before teaming up with him at The Oval at the top of the order in 1964 but he had consulted with some of the Yorkshire players before that Test match against Australia. 'John Hampshire said to me, "This so and so will block or pad up for five balls and off the last one he'll tuck it down to long leg for a single or he'll be running you out." I said to Geoffrey before that first Test together, "You can have half the bowling but I'm having the other half and if you think I'm going to stand there and watch you nudge the last ball for a single you can forget it because I won't run and I mean it."'

Boycott took note and they developed into a fine opening pair. On the tour to South Africa in the winter of 1964/65 Barber went out of his way to keep an eye on Boycott, to befriend him, to insist that he should join him on safaris, however reluctant his young partner was, and to stick up for him in a manner that few of the other England tourists were prepared to do. Barber also issued a forthright warning to the South African opening bowler, Peter Pollock (who had yet to show any signs that he would become an evangelical Christian), that there would be severe consequences if he continued to bowl any beamers at him – or his opening partner. 'He was like an older brother,' recalled Boycott. So perhaps I'll do Geoffrey a favour and put *Bob Barber: The Professional Amateur* by Colin Shindler alongside him.

Over the years Boycott took a fair amount of flak from Tony Greig, but they had some common ground as well. They both tended to say exactly what they thought, which in Greig's case in 1978 was 'His [Boycott's] ability to be where the fast bowlers aren't has long been a talking point among cricketers.' At the time Greig's view of Boycott may have been coloured by the fact that, having shown initial interest in joining the Packer 'Circus', Boycott eventually decided not to be part of it. Instead he became an unlikely pillar of the English cricketing establishment for a while, appearing in court as one of the TCCB's witnesses in the case resoundingly won by Packer. Moreover, two years earlier Greig – having succeeded Mike Denness as England captain – had tried to persuade Boycott to end his self-imposed exile from international cricket, albeit without success.

But Greig was not the sort to harbour grudges. Nor was he one to think long and hard before opening his mouth, which helps to explain his remarks before the Test series against the West Indies in 1976. 'You must remember that the West Indians, these guys, if they get on top they are magnificent cricketers. But if they're down, they grovel, and I intend, with the help of Closey and a few others, to make them grovel.' West Indies, no longer in need of any motivation from their captain, Clive Lloyd, won the series 3-0 and at The Oval Greig pretended to crawl on his hands and knees at the conclusion of the match.

Greig gave his brilliant team talk to the BBC on the roof of the pavilion at Hove – 'an interview I have never been allowed to forget' and 'a comment I have never attempted to defend'.

To be fair to him, he recognized his monumental error in front of the cameras on that day. 'Do I regret what I said?' he wrote years afterwards. 'Of course I do. There are times when you get things wrong and you have to admit it and accept the consequences.' Well said. Even so, let's pop Greig in between autobiographies of Michael Holding, who kept yorking him in that series, and Viv Richards, who has a long memory.

Meanwhile, the Gower autobiographies (two, so far) are alongside Graham Gooch's, with the sections on the Tiger Moth escapade well thumbed. This took place in Carrara, Queensland on the 1990/91 Ashes tour when Gooch was captain of England. During the most nondescript tour game imaginable on the Gold Coast, Gower could not resist hiring a Tiger Moth from a nearby airfield and buzzing the ground just as Robin Smith was reaching his century. He took with him an eager John Morris, a young batsman on his first – and last – tour, who had just completed his hundred in the match. To those of us looking on, this was a merry, harmless prank, a welcome diversion from a long and difficult tour with everyone miles from home and the Gulf War escalating fast. The tour management committee, which consisted of Gooch (the captain), Peter Lush (the tour manager), Micky Stewart (the team manager), and Allan Lamb (the vice-captain), could have dismissed this caper as a cheery little morale-boosting episode. Instead they fined Gower and the unfortunate Morris (Gower had offered a seat to the younger and much wiser Mike Atherton but he had declined) £1000, the maximum amount permitted – 'a bit steep in the era of deregulation,' observed Gower. Lamb, who was probably not one of the hawks on that tour committee, told Gower that at one point they were keen to send both miscreants home. At the time Gower was the leading run-scorer in the Tests by an alarming margin – he had scored 347 runs in three matches, having hit hundreds in Melbourne and Sydney. After Carrara and his draconian punishment, his form plummeted like a stone.

At the time the tour management's reaction seemed astonishing and misguided. It still does. Gower had the capacity to rile his captain – and it probably only needed a raised eyebrow to do it. Gooch could not understand how Gower operated and this must have exasperated him. Nor did Gower fit the work ethic that Micky Stewart advocated. But do not fall into the trap of thinking that Gower did not care or that he did not try. That may have been the case sometimes when he was playing for Leicestershire, but never for England – especially versus Australia, against whom he has a very fine record. Gower was always committed to playing Test cricket regardless of the venue or the lure of the rand, which did not apply to all his contemporaries. But Gooch and Stewart decided that they could not handle him, especially on tour; the sacrifice was too much for them, too damaging to the new team ethic. Eighteen months later Gower, contrary to his expectation after a conversation he'd had with Gooch earlier in the summer, was informed by his captain that he would not, after all, be going on the winter tour to India – ten minutes before the squad was announced on the radio. In the event, Gower did end up there, working for Sky TV. It was more fun watching him bat.

Captaincy is often a factor in fall-outs. One of the best books on my shelves is *Golden Boy* by Christian Ryan. It is about Kim Hughes and 'the bad old days of Australian cricket' and so much of the conflict that it covers hinges on the captaincy in the post-Packer world. The captaincy of Australia is often said to vie with the role of prime minister in importance in that country. When Greg Chappell was unavailable (after the Packer Affair he declined to tour much) they needed a new captain. Dennis Lillee was adamant that Rod Marsh should be the man in charge ahead of Hughes; Rod Marsh almost certainly thought Rod Marsh should be captain too. But Hughes – supremely gifted, blond, dashing, untainted by Packer, ambitious and incredibly naive – was asked to do the job. Understandably he was never going to refuse that offer.

So Australian cricket found itself with an unplayable lie. Marsh would have been a much better captain than Hughes but the Australian Cricket Board could not bring themselves to give him the job of leading the national side. Hughes, they decided, represented the brave new world. It must have been agony not only for Marsh and Lillee but ultimately for Hughes as well. Marsh – renowned as the ultimate team man – would not accept the offer of being vice-captain, and sometimes in the field he could barely hide his disgust at the latest Hughes decision, covering his face with his massive keeping gloves.

Lillee, meanwhile, kept bouncing Hughes in the nets – and in Perth the nets could be even quicker than the pitches in the middle at the WACA. Hughes kept hooking, seldom ducking, never complaining. And everyone looked on in amazement, frightened to say anything. So the bouncers kept coming. It is a riveting tale and at the end of it Hughes seems incredibly unembittered by the treatment he received from Marsh and

Lillee. If only they had made Marsh captain with Hughes in the team, watching and learning, possibly before taking on the job a few years later. But the fallout from the Packer Affair was too recent and too raw. And, in any case, Marsh was a wicketkeeper and they don't often captain Test sides well, you know (until the advent of M. S. Dhoni).

So *Golden Boy* will survive any downsizing and for the moment I'll surround this book with offerings from Lillee and Marsh – there are plenty to choose from. On past form Hughes won't mind that. Oddly this trio of West Aussies say they are still mates.

I'll stick the great tomes recounting the lives of Shane Warne and Steve Waugh together – teammates but hardly soulmates – and they might well occupy a shelf on their own. Waugh could be an intimidating cricketer towards the end of his career, but his autobiography is more intimidating still – at 801 pages long, a considerable deterrent to starting it even in lockdown. Waugh wrote every word of it, which suggests he may have intimidated his editor as well as everyone else. Warne's latest autobiography was, surprisingly, ghostwritten by Mark Nicholas since a ghostwriter usually prefers to remain anonymous. Nonetheless, Mark manages to capture Warne's voice adeptly.

Devon Malcolm's *You Guys are History* sits by Ray Illingworth's *One Man Committee*. Their relationship was never as productive as it should have been. While still playing, Illy was the shrewdest of shrewdies, who handled the differing characters of John Snow and Geoff Boycott well on the 1970/71 tour of Australia. But he was not so effective out of his whites when in a managerial role in later life, even if he managed to provide some great copy for those following England.

Ian Botham takes up a lot of space on my shelves. It is tempting to stick *Hitting Out: The Ian Chappell Story* (written in conjunction with Ashley Mallett) alongside Beefy. This is one feud that has never been resolved, which can only be a measure of the obstinacy of both men. I like both of them a lot. They have much in common and they should be mates, but they never will be after an ill-fated meeting in a bar in Melbourne in the winter of 1976/77. Many years ago, those running Channel Nine had the brainwave of putting them on air together during a Test match in Australia. They only did this once. They barely spoke a word to one another. So, instead of annoying both parties, perhaps I shall surround Botham with two intruders: *The Victorians: Twelve Titans who Forged Britain* and *The Churchill Factor* (though I'll have to acquire them first). The first of these was written by Jacob Rees-Mogg, the second by Boris Johnson, two Brexit-supporting Etonians in thrall to the boy from Buckler's Mead School in Yeovil, an ardent supporter of the Brexit project and now – thanks to Boris's patronage – Lord Botham of Ravensworth. I had not seen that coming when I plonked my kit next to his in the tiny shed behind the old pavilion at Taunton in 1974.

12

Somerset

'Still, there's always next year.'

Countless Somerset supporters

IT IS GETTING beyond a joke now. I played in a strong Somerset side four decades ago and I've followed some fine teams at Taunton since then, and still the Championship eludes us. I've tried to smile graciously at another near miss, to congratulate the worthy winners and to reel back from expounding on the sheer injustice of it all. Since 2001 Somerset have finished second six times in the Championship. In 2020 they made the final of the Bob Willis Trophy, a five-day game at Lord's at the end of September, and they lost – except that they didn't; the match was drawn but Essex won by virtue of a first-innings lead. Once again cricket was the winner, blah de blah de blah. And Somerset came second.

There are now just two sides who have definitely never won the County Championship: Northamptonshire and Somerset. We could have an argument about whether Gloucestershire should join this unhappy list... but I can't be bothered. They were reckoned to be at the top of the pile when W. G. Grace ruled the roost, but the Championship only acquired some form of official status in 1890. The Gloucestershire website tells me they were regarded as the Champion County in 1873, 1874, 1876 and 1877. To query that at the time would have prompted an argument with W. G., which may not have been an attractive proposition, and I'm in no mood to quibble about it now with our West Country cousins (well, almost) up in Bristol.

It was hard enough for Somerset to win a trophy of any description, let alone the Championship. I watched their attempt to win their first trophy, at Lord's in the Gillette Cup final of 1967, as a wide-eyed 12-year-old alongside my father in the Grand Stand. Naturally they lost valiantly. In 1978 I was in the team and Somerset clearly had a side capable of winning – mostly due to the presence of Richards, Garner and Botham – but in the final against Sussex we forgot our lines and were distraught.

I have a recollection of the great broadcaster, writer and adopted West Countryman, Alan Gibson, putting forward the notion around this time that he did not actually crave a Somerset victory in any competition, even though he was devoted to the team. He argued that it would somehow remove a delicious agony that had been part of the lives of Somerset cricket supporters for so many decades. (I notice that his son, Anthony, who now broadcasts on just about every red ball delivered or received by Somerset for the BBC on local radio, does not hold the same view with regard to the Championship.) At the time, I was puzzled by Alan's view. I understand it better now but still don't agree with it. Somerset have won their share of one-day trophies since 1979 (though there could have been many more), but the Championship is the most coveted trophy of all among the players (at least for the moment) and the supporters (for the last century or more) and we still have not won it, which has become a sore, scratched almost annually amid the winds and rain of late September. We have had enough of being lovable runners-up. Who remembers Ken Rosewall at Wimbledon? Well, obviously I do, but you get the drift. Time is ticking. Before long the Championship may not be worth winning. I'm not sure I have any false smiles left.

Under Brian Rose in the so-called 'glory' years, our best tilt at the Championship was in 1981; the West Indies were not touring so Richards and Garner were available for most of the matches; Botham, however, had a few distractions that summer but he still had time to play in nine of the twenty-two games, a statistic that is mind-boggling in the era of central contracts. Compared to recent years we did not get that close to winning the Championship in 1981, but at the time we definitely felt we were in the hunt when we began a match against Kent on 26 August. Three weeks earlier we had recorded our first victory on Yorkshire soil since 1902 and we were on a bit of a run.

The sun was shining at Folkestone and the pitch there looked as if it would suit Derek Underwood much as the glass slipper fitted Cinderella's foot. The toss would be important. We lost it so Kent's captain, Asif Iqbal, unhesitatingly chose to bat. We bowled them out for 186. Rose had summoned me early and was quickly rewarded with the wicket of Mark Benson; it was already starting to turn and I would end up bowling 25 overs in that innings, finishing with 3-48. All very satisfactory, but what would Derek Underwood do on here? I was conscious that here I was, still a relative novice of an off-spinner, pitted against one of England's finest slow(ish) bowlers. I actually liked the idea of that. Underwood had started bowling for England when I was eleven but he had to wait until his second Test match before Rohan Kanhai became the first of his 297 Test victims. Now I was his opposite number, which satisfied my vanity as well as being a source of some trepidation.

Underwood was 36 now but most definitely still a force. He would bowl a lot of overs at Folkestone, thanks to our top order but no thanks to me (bowled Johnson – that's Graham, an off-spinner – for 0). On that first evening, Underwood was introduced after five overs. Soon he bowled Jerry Lloyds, which heralded the arrival of Richards. Viv rarely took the canny view when facing international bowlers; instead he took the princely one. If they were the best in the world then they had to be subjugated. He actively wanted to face them just to demonstrate who was in charge – and who was the best batsman on the planet. Bob Willis was one of the Englishmen who endured the full force of Richards' bat. So was John Emburey a few years later, when his off breaks kept disappearing down the High Street in St John's, Antigua. (I remember telling Emburey that he should feel flattered by such an assault but this did not seem to console him greatly.)

By the same token, Richards relished the challenge of Underwood because Underwood was very good. Back in 1976 against Tony Greig's England, Viv had dominated him at The

Oval on a true pitch but here the odds were more in the spinners' favour. Viv counter-attacked brilliantly, driving 'Deadly' through mid-wicket as if batting on a flawless pitch. Such a shot should not have been possible on this surface. Underwood often wore a harassed look when bowling and this time his apprehension was real, but just before stumps he bowled Richards, who was furious with himself; Viv had been looking forward to renewing the contest in the morning so that he might stretch himself to the limit against the best once more.

With Viv gone, we felt it would be a struggle to go past Kent's total against Underwood (ably supported by Johnson), but Rose, Peter Roebuck and Peter Denning – three proud men of Somerset – found a way. Rose, using his pad as a second line of defence (and often a first, which was possible in those days before the DRS system came to the rescue of the dying breed of finger-spinners in the twenty-first century), batted for three and a half hours for 39. Roebuck was there for four hours for 51, often removing his bat from danger at the last millisecond against Underwood. Then there was Peter Denning, our left-hander from Chewton Mendip, who had never been regarded as a particularly good player of spin, one reason he had opened the batting for much of his career.

Denning was a brave, nuggety batsman, renowned for his 'Chewton Chop', which referred to a range of cut shots that – on a good day – sent the ball either side of the two third men who were often posted for him. Years earlier, in 1977 at Bath, Jeff Thomson had threatened to pin Denning to the sightscreen, so exasperated was he by the little left-hander's ability to cut just about any delivery heading in his direction.

He had some other shots as well but nobody noticed them. Denning outlasted everyone at Folkestone, scoring 98, most of which seemed to be tickled wide of first slip. This was a typically gutsy innings from a batsman who growled a lot and a cricketer as generous and selfless as any on the circuit. Dasher would take a quick single to the danger end when we were playing against the high-speed West Indians on the county circuit in the 1970s and 1980s, which was not universally the case.

Somehow Somerset had a lead of 123. Underwood had taken seven wickets but he had been compelled to bowl 54.4 overs to get them and they had cost 118 runs. The lead was enough to deflate Kent, especially after their first three batsmen departed for ducks in the second innings. I was busy again but must have remembered that on a turning pitch patience is the key. There was no need for cunning variations because the odds were already in my favour; eventually, if I kept landing it in the right place, the wickets would come. And so, after almost 30 overs, five of them did at a cost of 34 runs. Somerset had won by an innings and two runs.

It had been one of our better performances and I remember it more clearly than most since, for one game only, my figures had matched those of Underwood, one of England's greatest ever spinners, though you would not have guessed this was his status when bumping into him at the bar in the pavilion. Underwood hid his prowess and his fierce competitive streak well. Generally he would be found with a beer in one hand, a fag in the other and a self-deprecating smile on his lips. He would talk cricket happily, often seeking your opinion, yet this was the man with countless England caps, who had tormented the best. He was the antithesis of a top-class international sportsman until he set off on his run-up. He had a lean, muscle-free frame that did not suggest a natural athlete; his feet were forever splayed at ten to two, and even I might have challenged him in a twenty-yard dash. And yet he was world-class even though he once described himself as a 'low-mentality' bowler. He was reluctant to experiment too much, partly because he knew he could propel the ball onto a saucer at about 65 mph time and time again. Why jeopardize that? On a drying pitch he would be lethal with Alan Knott behind the stumps often leaping in the air to take the ball at shoulder height. In such conditions there was no escape for the batsmen. He was still a wonderful bowler on a dry surface, mainly because he gave you absolutely nothing to hit.

Knott went with Underwood as Marsh did with Lillee. Both appreciated the sublime skills of the other. The bowling of Underwood on a wet wicket allowed Knott to demonstrate his prowess behind the stumps. Knott was, of course, a quirky soul, who once told me about what he reckoned to be his finest ever session of wicketkeeping and it was indeed when Underwood was bowling. However, the spell he remembered was not on a venomous drying pitch when the ball was leaping skywards but when they were playing for England together on a true, dry surface in Lahore. He told me how Underwood bowled throughout the entire session in searing heat and then Knott said with a hint of pride, 'I didn't take a ball... but I was ready to take every one.' Underwood was that type of bowler and Knott that type of lateral thinker.

In 1976 I found myself batting at three for Somerset, believe it or not, against Underwood at Taunton. I cut him impishly for four behind square on the off side and was feeling pretty pleased with myself. I was only 21 and still merrily exploring what was possible. The ball had been a bit too straight and too full to cut but I did it anyway and the umpire signalled the boundary with a welcome flourish. Brian Rose was my partner and came down the pitch at the end of the over. 'Whatever you do, don't try that again,' he said. I must have tried to take note. A couple of overs later, in came Underwood and back I went again, but this time it was his arm ball, about 10 mph faster than usual and swinging in. My cut shot was not so effective this time. Just as I was about to complete it, the middle and off stumps were splattered and Rose's eyebrows headed northwards.

Underwood played for over twenty-five years and at the end he was just as ferociously committed as he was in 1963, scowling at himself if ever he delivered a poor ball, and relentlessly eager to add to his tally of wickets (which eventually totalled 2465 in first-class cricket). An even better example of his commitment came from his batting. He was not that gifted a batsman but he was incredibly brave. He always seemed to be the nightwatchman for England against the West Indies or Australia in the era before helmets. Lesser men hid in a cupboard at around 5.30 p.m. when the captain was casting around for a 'volunteer' to be nightwatchman, but not Deadly.

This was the man I (sort of) matched in one game at Folkestone all those years ago. After the win, the Somerset dressing room was buoyant ahead of the long drive west.

Perhaps this would be the year. Then, just before setting off for home, we put our ears to the radio for the cricket scores. Somehow Nottinghamshire and Sussex had won again. Even though we kept up our winning run, we could not catch them.

In 2010 Marcus Trescothick was given the Somerset captaincy. This was not quite such an automatic decision as one might imagine. By now he had withdrawn from international cricket after his mental health issues, which were highlighted by separation anxiety on another overseas tour, so there was risk attached to his appointment. But Brian Rose, the cricket director at Somerset, gave him the job and Trescothick responded to the task superbly.

He has always been a selfless cricketer and a guileless character, and he was regarded as the perfect vice-captain with England, forever keeping an eye on everyone in that dressing room. After he returned early from the England tour to India in 2006, the ECB – then headed by chairman Giles Clarke – were anxious to look after him. Clarke told me how upon his return they sent Marcus and his family off for a week to a remote and luxurious hotel in the middle of Devon, Bovey Castle, which seemed an ideal retreat with a lovely golf course. Months later the ECB were in touch with Trescothick to check how he was feeling and whether there was anything they could do to help. Clarke reported that Marcus's response was 'Wouldn't mind another week at Bovey Castle.'

I think Trescothick loved playing the game more than any professional cricketer I've come across. When he gave up in 2019, he hinted at that. 'I feel ready [to go] now. I was scared of it [retirement] for a long time and the prospect of seeking different employment. It was easier than expected to put my bat down as the coaching role took over.' It was as if there had been times when he could not cope without the prospect of playing cricket every April, but now there was a touch of realism and a way forward. 'I can't do it like I used to. I have to put my glasses on, for a start. It's not as easy as it used to be.'

For over two decades he was most comfortable in the middle, scratching away at the crease, before unveiling another glorious cover drive or pull shot. His withdrawal from international cricket at the age of 31 could have been a tragedy. In under seven years he had appeared in seventy-six Tests without being dropped but he might have played many more. However, he would display more bravery after his retirement from international cricket than during his time opening the batting for England against Courtney Walsh, Allan Donald or Brett Lee. In time he confronted his issues and he wrote about them in an excellent autobiography, *Coming Back to Me*, ghostwritten by Peter Hayter, who well understood what his subject was going through. There he reveals that his stay at Bovey Castle was, in fact, full of anxiety. After a false start in an ill-advised interview on Sky TV with Ian Ward, in which he referred to nothing more than a virus causing his sudden departure from India, he was prepared to speak openly in a matter-of-fact tone about his mental health problems. As a result, countless readers/listeners with similar issues were greatly encouraged by his candour and his honesty. If one of England's best sportsmen was prepared to open up about his depression – a taboo topic for so many – then why shouldn't the rest of us? He was taken aback by the impact his account of his illness had on others. Trescothick could hardly have achieved more if he had played another five years as an England cricketer.

By the end of Trescothick's first season in charge in 2010, Somerset were two points behind Nottinghamshire in the Championship table before their last game against Durham at Chester-le-Street. They had played some positive cricket along the way, with an ageing bowling attack, lots of runs from James Hildreth and Trescothick himself as well as a few sparkling innings from the 20-year-old Jos Buttler. There followed four excruciating days in September at Chester-le-Street, where I was wearing too many hats. At the time I was chairman of cricket at Somerset, which mostly meant having a few chats with my old captain, Brian Rose, who was now the cricket director, and saying to anyone within earshot, 'Carry on. You're all doing frightfully well,' in the manner of old Mr Grace (not W. G.). I was working for *Test Match Special*, who were covering the last round of Championship matches with the Somerset/Durham fixture as their focal point, and I was writing for the *Guardian*, all of which might be regarded as welcome relief at the end of an international summer that had soured. In the Lord's Test against Pakistan – unusually the last of the summer – the no-balling/spot-fixing furore involving Mohammad Asif, Mohammad Amir, the captain Salman Butt and undercover reporters from the *News of the World* was still thundering on.

Yet this innocent county game was hardly a tension-free escape from the international summer. Nottinghamshire, the main rivals, were playing against Lancashire at Old Trafford, where the rain kept falling more frequently than in

Durham, which gave Somerset their chance. It transpired that a Somerset victory would almost certainly be sufficient to take the title since, with restricted time available in Manchester, Nottinghamshire could realistically only accrue bonus points. Durham battled tenaciously throughout, even though they conceded a first-innings lead of 140. The old Somerset bowlers – mostly imports, unlike those in their recent sides – strained every sinew but time was running out as Durham scored 320 in their second innings, thanks to a century from the Australian, Michael Di Venuto. This left Somerset needing 181 for victory in 17 overs on the last afternoon, an almost impossible task though they flirted with it before settling for the points for a draw. Perhaps that would be enough.

With forty minutes of the season to go, Somerset were top of the table. The trophy was somewhere in the pavilion at Chester-le-Street, ready to be handed over to Trescothick and his team; so too was the backdrop for the presentation ceremony, which was decorated with all the sponsors' logos. But at Old Trafford the sun was out and Lancashire could do Somerset no favours. Nottinghamshire raced past 400 inside 90 overs in their first innings, which gave them maximum batting points and meant they had to take three Lancastrian wickets in the 17 overs remaining for a vital last bonus point. It took them just 4.4 overs to achieve that. So Nottinghamshire and Somerset ended up level on points, and Nottinghamshire were crowned the county champions, having registered one more victory throughout the season.

At the end of four exhausting days, I had to write this up for the *Guardian* after commiserating with Rose and one or two other Somerset stalwarts before setting off on the long journey south. Did Trescothick rail against the Lancastrians who had declared and lost against Nottinghamshire on 27 August and who could neither restrict Chris Read's team to less than 400 in their final match nor find three or four batsmen capable of batting anything like 17 overs? Of course he didn't.

'We were not quite good enough,' said Trescothick. 'It's gutting. We knew we would have been the first team ever to do it from Somerset and we knew how special that would have been. We will have to wait until next year. It feels terrible and it could take a long time to get over this.' So there were no celebrations, just that welling feeling accompanied by a mixture of pride and admiration for this Somerset team and, in particular, their captain.

Three days later Somerset lost a day/night final at Lord's – a terrible idea, swiftly abandoned – to Warwickshire. Earlier in the season they had already been runners-up in the T20 final at Southampton, losing to Hampshire amid considerable chaos, with the scores level. Those defeats were hard to take but it was the Championship that everyone wanted.

They still wanted it in 2016. By mid-season, now led by the Australian Chris Rogers, Somerset were fretting about relegation; by the end of the summer, having decided to play on more sporting, bowler-friendly pitches, they had another chance to win the trophy. Their final game was against Nottinghamshire at Taunton and I was there again with all my hats on. They defeated Nottinghamshire by 325 runs in three days. The pitch helped the spinners yet Somerset scored 678 runs for the loss of 16 wickets in the game; Dom Bess – in the second

Championship outing of his life – took 5-43 in the first innings, while Jack Leach took 8-113 in the match. It was an utterly straightforward victory against a side already doomed to relegation. And yet Somerset squandered their chances of winning the pennant on the first day. In the final session they were coasting on 302-2, with Rogers and James Hildreth at the crease with hundreds to their name. By the close they were 322-9. At one point they managed to lose five wickets without scoring a run.

There are always arcane equations come the last game of the season, and it transpired that if Somerset had scored 400 in their first innings against Nottinghamshire, gaining maximum batting points, this would have ruled out the possibility of Yorkshire being able to win the Championship and that would have made a significant difference. Yorkshire were at Lord's, where Middlesex began their final game at the top of the table. If on the final day Yorkshire had been unable to win the Championship it is very unlikely they would have been interested in contriving a game on a moribund track where wickets were hard to come by. But now they were very interested. If they could win, a remarkable heist for the Tykes was on the cards.

On that final day James Franklin, the Middlesex captain, negotiated well and, after some declaration bowling, he could set an enticing target on the proviso that Yorkshire 'went all the way'. A draw was no good to either side. Despite a first-innings deficit of 120, Middlesex – having set their opponents 240 to win in 40 overs – won by 61 runs, with Toby Roland-Jones finishing it all off in the last hour of the season with a hat-trick.

Unusually on the scheduled fourth day, I was required to go to Taunton even though no cricket was being played there since Somerset had already won their game and were therefore sitting pretty – though not secure – at the top of the table by twelve points. I live about forty-five minutes from the ground and on the drive there Middlesex scored about 140 runs. The joke bowlers were setting up the agreed target for Yorkshire and hearts were already sinking at the County Ground.

All three bars at Taunton were full. It was still possible that Somerset might be crowned champions at the end of the day, and the televisions were on for the masochists to watch what was happening up at Lord's. There was much grumpiness in evidence and a feeling of foreboding. 'No way to play the game,' murmured disgruntled locals. Matthew Maynard, the Somerset coach, was more realistic: 'As far as I'm concerned, it's well within the spirit of the game. Both sides had to win and in their position we would have done something similar,' he said.

The players wandered around the ground helplessly. James Hildreth, with a broken right ankle having been hit by a yorker early in his brilliant innings on the first day, was on crutches. The chief executive, Guy Lavender, decided he needed a beer. Marcus Trescothick played football with his daughters on the outfield and was later joined by a few colleagues who did not want to follow the melodrama on the TV. Then Toby Roland-Jones finished it all off at Lord's with that hat-trick; the Taunton outfield emptied, so too the bars and the stomachs. Somerset, who had attracted so much pious ire for having the temerity to contrive some pitches that brought the spinners right back into the game (and ultimately to offer up two spinners for England in Leach and Bess), had to be gracious in defeat. Again.

At the weekend I wrote for the *Observer* not so much about Somerset's angst but the consuming drama that the end of the season had generated. County cricket was, briefly, sexy. 'The Championship is still the trophy that means the most and somehow that has happened without millions of pounds being spent on delivering the "right brand to the cricketing con-sumer". By way of contrast get ready for an onslaught from the marketeers when the ECB launches its new T20 competition.'

Here in September 2016 was an early reference to the plans for a second short-form competition that would eventually morph into The Hundred and that, as I write, has yet to take place. Back then I was already very gloomy about the devastation that a second short-form competition between contrived city clubs with no genuine support base might cause to the domestic schedule. 'Hopefully all of you outside of Yorkshire and Somerset enjoyed the tension and drama of the final round because this may soon become a relic of the past,' I wrote. 'We are in real danger of sleepwalking into chaos. We could soon have a domestic structure that diminishes the Championship significantly. The debate over the proposals for a new T20 competition in addition to the existing NatWest Blast is coming to a head. It seems as if it is no longer a battle of reasoned arguments, but a battle of wills and egos, with self-interest rather than common sense dictating the outcome. At the last meeting the vote was not so much on the merit of the proposals, but a "back me or sack me" resolution from the centre. Which may not be the best way to plot the future.' The new tournament has yet to surface and nothing has happened in the intervening five years to make me change my view of it. One of its enthusiastic supporters, Colin Graves, the chairman of the ECB in 2016, was backed and not sacked but has now moved on. Yet his legacy, The Hundred, is due to lurch into action in July 2021, out of kilter with the modern game before it has started.

Most recently, Somerset's Championship sagas have involved Essex and in particular Trescothick's replacement in the England side, Alastair Cook. In 2019 there was another showdown at Taunton in late September, which – as the schedulers probably acknowledge but then ignore – is actually deep into autumn and not the best time to try to play cricket. The wind and rain lashed onto the open-air balcony of Somerset's latest pavilion where the *TMS* team was assembled. We dug out our thermals and ski jackets and duly reported the 158 overs of play that were possible in between the squalls during the four days. The wicket took turn – a lot of turn – and it was on the edge. Still, Cook could bat on it. He occupied the crease for 68 overs in the match and was out once for a total of 83 runs. For Somerset it was an ugly race against time, allied to the fear that they might be penalized points for a poor playing surface. Given the terrible forecast, they needed a fast game and, of course, a victorious one. Somerset scored 203. At one point Essex were 102-1 in reply – so impossible was the wicket – but after the dismissal of Cook they collapsed to 141 all out. By now, after all the foul weather, there were only ninety minutes of play left. So Somerset's captain, Tom Abell, preposterously yet logically forfeited his side's second innings and sent Essex back in when the visitors in effect needed 63 to win from about 18 overs. Cook was still there at the end with Essex on 45-1 and the match was drawn. More handshakes, more congratulations to the victors, more exasperation, more gloomy resignation.

If nothing else, Cook had highlighted why he was better than everyone else and how he had retained his unswerving commitment to Essex. He had given up playing for England in September 2018, after which there was a simple logic to his cricketing plans. He may have been exhausted by the demands of international cricket but he still liked batting and he still enjoyed the buzz of the Essex dressing room so he continued to play. Cook has always known his own mind and he is generally reluctant to change it. A couple of examples: back in 2009 when he was still a relatively junior member of the England team, we were chatting at a function and he opined that there were too many counties. I understood that argument; I could just about agree with it, especially if we could be transported to a situation where we were able to start with a blank sheet of paper, but in a world-weary way I asked how any revamp could completely ignore more than a hundred years of tradition. How do you decide which counties have to go? 'Easy,' he said, 'just chop off those who are currently at the bottom of the second division.' Well, there was a certain logic to that but I could not resist pointing out that this would mean the end of Surrey and Middlesex as first-class counties since they were hovering in the lower reaches of the second division at the time.

A few years later Cook was England captain and we briefly broached the sensitive subject of Kevin Pietersen and his exile from the England team. I congratulated him on his pragmatism and vision, having been appointed captain after Andrew Strauss, to bring him back for the England tour to India in 2012, where Pietersen (and Cook himself) played some brilliant innings that led to a rare series victory on Indian soil. 'I wouldn't have picked him if I'd had my way,' he said. Pietersen's behaviour to Strauss at the end of 2011 had made up Cook's mind – and Cook does not change his mind easily. He has always been so much tougher than those choirboy looks suggest.

Fast-forward to 2019 and Cook, almost inevitably, topped the Essex batting averages by a considerable margin on surfaces at Chelmsford that were hardly more conducive to heavy run-scoring than those at Taunton. The highest score by any of Essex's opponents at Chelmsford that season was Kent's 224 at the end of May. (The highest by any of Somerset's opponents at Taunton throughout that summer was Surrey's 380.) Two months after the game at Taunton, Somerset were docked twelve points to be carried forward to the next Championship season, which turned out to be 2021, along with a twelve-point suspended sentence. Who knows what the authorities would have done if Somerset had won that match against Essex to take them to the top of the table? For certain, the ECB could not have waited another two months to come to their decision.

So the two teams all shook hands before Essex received the trophy. Among them was Trescothick in his last season, who had not played in the Somerset first team for two months. He had already announced his retirement and had been helping the coaching staff in the second half of the season, but on this day he had made sure he had his whites with him. He had spent the last few hours of his life as a professional cricketer as a drinks carrier in his faded old Somerset cap (though far from his first one in all those years at the club). Then at 5.15 p.m., out he came in pristine whites as a substitute fielder, clutching a helmet before fielding at bat/pad or falling to his knees in the gully to the spinners. Seldom has a sub received such an ovation. At the end he led the players from the field and the Essex team lined up to bid him farewell.

Trescothick was an official member of the coaching staff when the teams met again twelve months later while Cook was still opening the batting for his beloved Essex. This time the venue was Lord's, the duration of the game was five days and the Bob Willis Trophy was at stake. In a hastily arranged tournament to ensure some red-ball cricket in a Covid-ravaged summer, Essex and Somerset had demonstrated throughout August and early September that they were still the two best red-ball teams in the country by qualifying convincingly for the final. Both were unbeaten in the competition and it stayed that way... but Essex would win the trophy.

The matches were played behind closed doors and streamed on the increasingly sophisticated county websites and else-where. This time I was wearing just two hats, working for the *Guardian* and *TMS*. I had long since left the position of cricket chairman at Somerset, meaning I could rail against the advent of The Hundred without compromising the county, which, like many others, had become more amenable to the tournament with the promise of £1.3m per annum if they agreed to the proposals. The club members were not so sure about the new competition. They were supposed to be enthusiastic about supporting a team called Welsh Fire who were to play all their games in Cardiff; in reality, they were probably no more enamoured by this prospect than I was.

So on 23 September I joined the media contingent in the Tavern for my first visit of the summer to Lord's. The usual press box was out of bounds since the builders were at work on the Compton and Edrich Stands. This made me feel old. In my first year as a journalist I had been at Lord's for the famous Test against India as Gooch posted 333 when those two stands were being built. As in 1990, there were therefore shorter boundaries at the Nursery End but in 2020 no one could exploit them as spectacularly as Kapil Dev did when batting against Eddie Hemmings in that run-soaked England victory. The runs did not come so readily in 2020. In fact, Somerset slipped up in their first innings in a similar manner to when they played Nottinghamshire in 2016. They had recovered tenaciously after a stuttering start to 266-5, whereupon they were bowled out for 301. The collapse was not so rapid as the one against Nottinghamshire but it had the same consequences. For this match it had been decided that, if the contest was drawn, the side with a first-innings lead would prevail. In the end – against the odds – the match was drawn. Some play was lost to rain on the first two days and the pitch was sluggish. It was hard work to take wickets or to score freely except for a couple of left-handed opening batsmen.

There was, of course, no one there except the players, their support staff, the broadcasters and writers and the odd long-suffering steward seeking shelter. Throughout the last four days there was a biting wind; it was cold in the Tavern boxes, where some of us committed the heinous sin of opening the windows (as health and safety required) and putting on the radiators; it was colder still for the players out on the field unless they had the good fortune to be batting or bowling, and ultimately it was bloody freezing for the two umpires, Rob Bailey and Russell Warren, who had to be out there all the time. The match was streamed here, there and everywhere but there was not a spectator in sight. And yet it was a compelling game of cricket in which both sets of players gave their all throughout. Both teams were desperate to win a new, beautifully designed trophy that managed to capture the essence of Bob Willis in his delivery stride. In the end I had to file yet another report of a Somerset near miss: 'Don't ask me to explain to a non-cricket lover how I have been consumed by a contest that lasted for five days, which finished as a draw and yet one of the teams, Essex, ended up winning the trophy. It has not been a normal summer of cricket, but I guess that we should be grateful that there has been any cricket at all.'

One of the two left-handed opening batsmen to catch the eye was Tom Lammonby of Somerset: 20 years of age and purring to his third first-class century in the six games he had played in the competition. At Lord's he had begun his second innings of the match on a pair. And then, with a hint of the impishness and a touch of the feline grace that character-ized my old England colleague Graeme Fowler, he sped to a century, timing the ball better than anybody else in the match – except Cook.

I had never seen Cook bat so freely. In the first innings he scored 172 out of Essex's total of 337-8. While he was at the crease, only 94 runs had come from elsewhere. It was his cover driving that grabbed the attention. He has always clipped the ball away off the legs impeccably; his pull and cut shots seemed a natural response but often his cover drives lacked the same fluency. Sometimes in a taxing Test match he did not bother with the stroke. This was not the case at Lord's in 2020, where – almost for the first time – I was marvelling at the elegance of his batting. Initially I thought this might have been a reaction to watching Dominic Sibley and Rory Burns through the Test summer of 2020. By comparison, Cook could be considered Goweresque. But instead I came to realize that here was a batsman at peace with the world, simply trusting a technique that had served him so well for almost two decades. Despite the isolation, this was a magnificent innings. Cook, the Masterchef. It was all so simple. He was happy just to watch the ball and react. Trescothick, looking on alongside the rest of Somerset's backroom staff, would have recognized that feeling better than most.

Afterword

I STARTED ALL this in Lockdown One and I'm finishing it in Lockdown Three. When I set off I was an employee of the *Guardian*; now I'm what I fancifully call a freelancer. When I started, Washington DC might have been regarded as the bastion of the free world. As I write, they are storming the Capitol there. In London the NHS is under greater pressure than at any time in the Covid crisis. Somehow the make-up of England's bowling attack for the first Test against Sri Lanka in Galle does not seem to amount to a hill of beans in this crazy world. But I have been keeping an eye on that anyway.

I left the *Guardian* and the *Observer* – amicably – at the end of 2020. Covid induced the need for some late cuts in the sport department; the *Guardian* offered incentives to go and I went. I'm aware that I may not be a natural freelancer. If so I won't be the only ex-Somerset cricketer in this category. When I was a player the press box at Taunton was the undisputed domain of Eric Hill, who had been a professional at the club from 1947 to 1951, an active and progressive committee man and captain of the second team as well as being a reporter on Somerset cricket for over four decades. He ruled the roost in the old press box and, when a new one was eventually built at Taunton, it was appropriately named after Eric, who was never quite as stern as he looked. He was one of the old school and his contemporary at school in Taunton, the polymath Alan Gibson, wrote this about him: 'He rules over the tatty old press box at Taunton with what purports to be an iron glove, though there is a velvet hand within it. He will growl about "you cowboys" to visitors who arrive late and want to borrow his scorecard, but having been suitably humbled they get their information and their telephone calls in the end... He rightly dislikes a stream of dirty stories in a press box... but I have noticed he is becoming increasingly voluble himself. Last season I heard him mutter "Good shot" twice in one over.'

Why has Eric sprung to mind? Because he is the only freelancer I've come across who made a point of going ex-directory. I haven't gone that far but it has seldom been my natural instinct to go looking for work, which I gather is what freelancers are supposed to do.

The mechanics of reporting the game have changed radically since Eric's time. I just caught the latter stages of the old system, which operated when county press boxes were more crowded than they are today. The mobile phone was still being developed, as was the laptop. So, upon arrival at the various press boxes around the counties, the tentative newcomer had a few anxious moments. It was important not to sit in the space that had been established as the territory of the local reporter for decades past. Having taken one's seat, it was probably better not to pontificate about the state of the game/nation too vehemently; my off breaks were better than theirs but not my journalistic skills. Moreover, this upstart had skipped all the hard yards required for becoming a cricket correspondent just by playing the game and penning the odd column as a hobby. It was imperative to negotiate access to the solitary telephone in the box in order to ring through copy towards the end of the day. Finally there was the hurdle of delivering the piece in the cramped confines of the press box usually to a deaf copy-taker in Wakefield, who required every stilted phrase to be repeated two or three times in front of an audience that could hardly be described as admiring.

Similarly, on winter tours the hardest part was not writing the reports but getting them back to the sports desk. It was no longer necessary to traipse down to the telex office. Peter Smith of the *Daily Mail* and the leader of the press pack in the 1980s explained to me back then how he could never relax until he had received confirmation that his copy had landed. Once, when touring India, he was especially concerned about the telex facilities in Jammu in the north of the country. 'Do not worry, sir. We have four machines at the ground,' he was told. It transpired that these four machines comprised two men and two bicycles.

When I set off as a correspondent there was an embryonic portable computer called a Tandy in use, which could send copy electronically – with a bit of luck and a lot of leads. Meanwhile, getting a reliable phone line in parts of the Caribbean or India was often impossible. However, given my IT ignorance, I started with just a pad of paper and a pen in my bag and the hope in my heart that a telephone would somehow connect me to the copy-takers towards the end of the day. By comparison, that part of the job is a breeze now. The mobile phone and the laptop soon became game-changers.

These instruments also contributed to a substantial change in the behaviour of cricket writers in their press boxes. For the journalist, the mobile phone allowed easy access to the copy-takers for a little while longer until they were no longer required; then it presented the swiftest route to KP's Twitter account, which was obviously regarded as essential reading, and also to the sports desk, who sometimes had some bright ideas to pass on. My colleague on the *Guardian*, Ali Martin, probably has more conversations with the desk in one day than Mike Selvey had on an entire tour of Australia. The mobile phone's ubiquity was not necessarily as beneficial to the players. Ian Botham was, at least, spared the prospect of being snapped by a mobile phone's camera on a night out back in the 1980s, a luxury denied Ben Stokes three decades later. As a player Botham did not have the opportunity to tweet and he was surely none the worse for that.

Enter a press box at a Test match today and the rows of correspondents sit there earnestly in front of their laptops, which are always open and active. They may also be wearing earpieces from which they can choose to listen to the sages of Sky TV or *Test Match Special* just in case something interesting or newsworthy has been said. Even at 11.01 a.m. the box has become a place of work as fingers tap away on silent keyboards (although they may just as easily be booking up their holidays rather than researching the number of times Dominic Sibley has been caught down the leg side in Test cricket).

When the TV cameras swing around to the dressing rooms, open laptops are often in evidence there as well. We can never be sure what the players are doing, but the assumption is that a batsman who has recently returned to the pavilion is watching footage of his dismissal in a desperate bid to analyse the mistake and to work out ways to correct it. This was not possible when I began playing professionally. I had no real idea what I looked like at the crease. If the game was being televised I would be keen to watch the highlights, only to be disappointed that – out of a vitally important innings of 37 – just one shot was replayed in the highlights package. Maybe it was that exquisite stroke for four, which had felt like a mixture of Colin Cowdrey and Barry Richards in their pomp. Presumably it would look something like that as well. Then came the numbing deflation as I witnessed a cover drive more reminiscent of a novice lumberjack hacking down a particularly stubborn oak.

Now I can't imagine what we did all day in the press box before the advent of the laptop. I guess we must have just sat there and watched the cricket – quite carefully. There was no big screen offering the chance to watch the wicket that fell just as I was pouring a cup of coffee; even the TV replays, once televisions had been placed in the box, were less frequent and less reliable back then. (The memory of Denis Compton on black-and-white TV, shouting 'Oh my goodness, he's got another one out' after a rare TV replay was shown, still cheers me up.) So we may have had to concentrate a little harder on the game as we chatted and gossiped and made the odd note. In the days of Cornhill's sponsorship of Test cricket, we waited patiently for the trays bearing goblets of wine that were offered and, more often than not, gratefully received around lunchtime. There would be a constant hum of conversation until about 4.30 p.m., when there might be the odd request for the noise level to abate as tomorrow morning's columns were conjured up.

Having a drink during the game has long since disappeared, as has the popular bar at the back of the old press box at The Oval. For the professionals in the press or commentary boxes, sipping alcohol during the hours of play has become as rare as watching a batsman taking guard in a cap or a slow handclap rippling around the ground because of the turgid progress of the game. It's probably just ill-conceived nostalgia that has me pining for a slow handclap. I have not witnessed one this century. Like spotted dick, the reality isn't worth revisiting. Even so, what is the world coming to? Batsmen just do not know how to bore like they used to. If ever there's a lull in play now, there may be the brief diversion of a Mexican wave or the bouncing of a beach ball around the stand to goad the stewards or the construction of a snake from empty plastic beer glasses... but there is no slow handclap.

This is partly because modern Test cricket has fewer dull moments than ever before. The draw has become a rare event, something else to savour. As I write, Joe Root has led England sixty-one times in Test cricket, winning twenty-seven matches and drawing nine. What a contrast to the 1960s, an era that some look back on with misty-eyed reverence as Tom, Colin, Lord Ted and M. J. K. gleaned so many enchanting runs and the overs were bowled so quickly. Bear in mind that Colin Cowdrey drew fifteen of the twenty-seven matches when he was captaining England; M. J. K. Smith drew seventeen out of twenty-five. This was not such a wonderful time for cricket after all.

Geoffrey Boycott and Ken Barrington were both dropped for slow scoring in Test cricket, which was often played out in front of meagre crowds. The authorities agonized over how to improve the game. In fact, they reacted with rather more speed than their fuddy-duddy image might suggest possible: they introduced a one-day tournament, which became the Gillette Cup; they permitted and encouraged the signing of players from overseas, which resulted in the best player in the world, Garry Sobers, adorning our county grounds; and they sanctioned the 40-over Sunday League – all in the space of half a dozen years. And for good measure they abolished the ludicrous distinction between gentlemen and players.

Test cricket is different now. Argue among yourselves whether it is better, but it is undoubtedly more action-packed, and in the UK (but sadly not in the rest of the world) many more spectators pay much more money to come and watch it. Meanwhile, the crowds still flock to the white-ball formats. We do not need a bastardized version of T20 – but we won't go there again.

For all the changes – or maybe because of some of the changes – it is still a magnificent game. In this century, batsmen play more shots than they used to and they have invented about half a dozen new ones. In the mid-1980s I wrote a coaching guide for the TCCB, in which the unknown teenagers Mike Atherton and Mark Ramprakash were the models for all the line drawings, demonstrating all the cricket strokes available to a young batsman. The reverse sweep barely got a mention and there was nothing about the switch hit, the ramp, the scoop or the helicopter shot. Nor could an eager young bowler read much about reverse swing and nothing at all about the knuckle ball, the slower ball bouncer, the carrom ball or the wide yorker. (I'm still unsure about the benefits of that one.) I struggled to find a wrist-spinner to explain the intricacies of his art. Now they are everywhere, especially when a white ball is involved. Cricketers have become more curious and more eager to explore the limits of their talent. This must be good news.

Yet, despite all the changes, the fundamentals of what makes a great batsman or bowler remain the same. By the same token, a Test match heading to an unknown climax on the fifth day is still a riveting, multi-layered drama that few other sporting contests can match. With or without the scoops, the ramps and the knuckle balls, a World Cup final can deliver mesmerizing melodrama. We only have to go back to 2019 to be reminded of the game's capacity to captivate and enthral.

In the winter of 2021/22 England set off for Australia once more and we were all beguiled by the prospect of another Ashes series, especially amid the gloom of Covid. The usual pattern was followed – the players, the press, the fans of the northern hemisphere conjure up a remarkable amount of optimism to convince themselves that the time has come. Then, on the toughest tour of all, England's cricketers wilt not only against the pacemen of Australia but also the collective will of a nation. That has now been the outcome on eight of the last nine Ashes tours.

Joe Root joined a very select band of Englishmen to lead two expeditions to Australia. By November 2021 we may well have convinced ourselves that the Ashes could be regained under his leadership as RC Robertson Glasgow's famous query – 'Who ever hoped like a cricketer?' – resurfaced. By January 2022 we could only ask why we had been so gullible.

I had to adjust to the fact that I was unable to be in Australia for the Ashes for the first time since 1979 and yet the series went ahead anyway. Not many cricketers are indispensable; I'm not sure any journalists are, but occasionally we need that reminder. In any case, after leaving the *Guardian* I've received my leaving presents: generous gifts of wine plus a witty back-page spoof from the sports desk in which newshound/correspondent extraordinaire Ali Martin, for the first time in his life, begins a news story with the word 'Well'. (He thinks I began too many of my news stories – and there weren't many of those – with a 'Well, who would have thought it...?') There was also a Neville Cardus exclusive, revealing that there was about to be a swoop for my services by the ECB since they wanted someone to spearhead their public relations blitz ahead of the launch of The Hundred. Thanks to the generosity of my colleagues in the press box, I acquired an unusually expensive golf club, which was bound to result in my handicap coming down by at least two shots – though curiously this has yet to happen.

However, I hope to still be around occasionally so that I can dispense words of wisdom to the young pups who now inhabit the press box. I now realize I have been fortunate enough for the vast majority of my working life to have – unwittingly – followed guidance that was given by one of the great writers for the *Observer*. It came from Katharine Whitehorn and it is worth repeating: 'The best careers advice to the young is to find out what you like best and to get someone to pay you for doing it.'

Acknowledgements

For the second time in two years I'd like to thank Clare Drysdale, the editorial director at Allen & Unwin in London and Anna Marks in Devon for their guidance and encouragement throughout three lockdowns.

Index